Buffers

GUIDE TO

SURFING

CRAIG JARVIS

© Haynes Publishing 2019
Published May 2019

A CIP Catalogue record for this book
is available from the British Library.

ISBN: 978 1 78521 556 8 (print)
      978 1 78521 615 2 (eBook)

Library of Congress control no. 2018952721

Published by Haynes Publishing,
Sparkford, Yeovil, Somerset BA22 7JJ
Tel: 01963 440635
Int. tel: +44 1963 440635
Website: www.haynes.com

Printed in Malaysia.

Bluffer's Guide®, Bluffer's® and Bluff Your Way®
are registered trademarks.

Series Editor: David Allsop.
Front cover illustration by Alan Capel.

CONTENTS

Understand the culture, get to grips with what is cool and what is not, grasp a smattering of the terminology, learn how to bluff your way out of ever having to go for a surf, and you're made.

SURF'S UP

As you read these words, grubby and bearded feral surfers are stumbling along foreign shores searching for the perfect wave. Every male surfer yearns to find his own secret point break on a remote beach, along with a beautiful island girl dressed in nothing but a G-string of coconut pith. Ideally she'll have an indulgent and largely absent father who owns a nearby brewery.

Every female surfer yearns to find a bronzed Adonis who surfs like a god, is utterly faithful, and has an ailing billionaire guardian who dotes on him and has no close family. Very few surfers live their dreams.

There are those (predominantly men) who travel around with boards strapped to their car roofs, pretending to unsuspecting onlookers (mainly the cute ones in bikinis) that they are surfers. They understand nothing of the history of surfing, the culture and etiquette of the sport, or which way a surfboard is supposed to go in the water (the pointy bit goes at the front). These people are often referred to as 'highway surfers'. The difference between a highway surfer and a bluffer is a fine line, but by the end of this guide you will know exactly where that line is drawn.

Surfing is a difficult sport requiring years of hard work to acquire the minimum level of competency. Bluffers do not have years to spare, yet might find themselves needing to take a view on whether or not luminous wetsuits are still the thing (they're not) or whether hardcore surfers should always have a shaggy dog with them at the beach (undecided, so plenty of mileage there). This is because surfing has just as much to do with the culture that surrounds it as it does with actually riding a wave. This suits the bluffer to perfection. Understand the culture, get to grips with what is cool and what is not, grasp a smattering of the terminology, learn how to bluff your way out of ever having to go for a surf, and you're made.

This short but definitive guide sets out to conduct you through the main danger zones encountered in surfing discussions, and to equip you with a vocabulary and an evasive technique that will minimise the risk of being rumbled as a bluffer. It will give you a few easy-to-learn hints and techniques designed to allow you to be accepted as a surfer of rare ability and experience. But it will do more. It will provide the tools to impress legions of marvelling listeners with your knowledge and insight – without anyone discovering that before reading it you didn't know the difference between 'dropping in' and 'going over the falls' (neither of which you are advised to attempt).

MAKING A SPLASH

Surfing, first observed and recorded by a junior officer on Captain Cook's ill-fated third expedition to the Pacific in the late 1770s, has its roots in Hawaii.

Some say that it started earlier in Peru, but there is no proof of this. So you're advised to stick to Hawaii, where it was the sport of kings. Men, women, girls and youths all surfed together, but Hawaiian royalty frequently reserved the best beaches for themselves. When the surf was up, everyone dropped whatever they were doing and went surfing. Much like today then, except in Hawaii it was done in the nude – on boards made from koa wood (for the hoi polloi) and from the aptly named wiliwili tree (for chiefs).

Unfortunately (or rather, fortunately for some), nude surfing often led to things like nude frolicking in the waves and, inevitably, casual sex. In the early 1800s Protestant missionaries frowned upon such unspeakable behaviour and put a stop to it on the grounds that it was clearly far too much fun. Surfing went down the tubes, so to speak, for 100 years, until American writer Jack London arrived in Hawaii in 1907.

Despite trying to 'surf-ride' for hours on end at Waikiki beach, London could not grasp the fundamentals of the sport and chose to write about it instead, making him the first surfing bluffer. Here's a sample of what he had to say about the waves:

The mere struggle with them, facing them and paddling seaward over them and through them, was sport enough in itself. You had to have your wits about you, for it was a battle in which mighty blows were struck, on one side, and in which cunning was used on the other side – a struggle between insensate force and intelligence.

It was Hawaiian surfer Duke Kahanamoku, already a five time US Olympic swimming medallist, who took to the waves with his board around the same time and made riding them a sport. He proved himself to be highly skilled at it, despite the fact that he wore an extraordinary, genital-squeezing, hybrid Speedo/T-shirt one-piece swimsuit which must have severely hampered his style. Duke became known as the father of modern surfing, and took it and his costume from Hawaii to show to the world as part of his travelling swimming exhibitions. His surfing exhibition at Sydney's Freshwater Beach in 1914 is widely regarded as a seminal event in the development of surfing in Australia.

BOARD BASICS

It is imperative for bluffers to be able to participate in discussions that include topics like swell direction, tides, wave sizes, how to 'snake' and get away with it, and the virtues of a frontside air reverse as opposed to full rail carving (*see* Glossary). You don't need to know much more than their names, but before you commit any of them to memory, you need some understanding of the surfboards themselves – how they are supposed to work and what motivates the people who create them. Knowing something about the people who actually make the boards (known as 'shapers') is an important component in the bluffer's bank of recyclable information because shapers are generally very reclusive. This is usually because they are either socially inept, paranoid or on the run because someone really is looking for them – i.e., the police or a jealous husband.

BOARD DEVELOPMENT
Essentially, a surfboard is made by taking a chunk of

foam (known as a 'blank'), shaping it (either by machine or by hand), covering it with fibreglass and then sealing it with resin – unless it is made from wood and coated with oil, for those who really want to get back to basics.

These days there are many different methods of constructing surfboards with new, experimental materials. Some of them work; some of them result in boards that would be best accompanied by a steam iron, or boards with dimples the size of golf balls, or boards so heavy they can only be picked up by a forklift. These are usually sold to beginners for large amounts of money.

Surfing, at its core, consists of a surfer, a surfboard and a wave. These are the three intrinsic elements, and everything else, from board shorts and bikinis to wetsuits and wax, are just accessories.

Surfboards first came out without any fins or 'skegs' (the surfboard 'keels'), but a legendary American surfer called Tom Blake put a stop to that in 1935 and a whole new fad started. It was very obvious that the boards performed better with a fin, but would one fin be better than two, or two fins better than three? Australian Mark Richards won four world titles on a twin-fin surfboard between 1979 and 1982. Another Australian, Simon Anderson, put three fins on his, called it a Thruster, won contests with it, forgot to copyright his design and, consequently, is not as rich as he should be.

Many, like Nathan Fletcher and Anthony Tashnick, two of the more famous American big wave pro surfers, prefer a four or 'quad-fin' set-up, while the popular underground 'Bonzer' surfboard incorporates five. For the bluffer, the most common configuration is three fins. To get into technical talk about the superiority of the quad-fin or the 'down-the-line speed' of the twin-fin would be courting disaster. All you need to know is that the three-fin set-up is faster and has more drive than the others. You might perhaps speculate about a future for a 'sextufin' (six) set-up, or suggest that we're all headed for surfing in the buff again and really going back to basics – so the size and number of fins will become completely irrelevant.

SHAPERS

The Chinese, with their cheap 'pop-out' boards (ones that come off a factory production line), may be hell-bent on taking over global board production, but traditional board shapers are still among the most important people in the surfing world. Why? Because they surf, and thus they tend to know what type of board suits what type of surfer.

Surfing, at its core, consists of a surfer, a surfboard and a wave. These are the three intrinsic elements, and everything else, from board shorts and bikinis to wetsuits and wax, are just accessories.

The surfboard shaper can make you a better surfer or a worse surfer. Your level of skill depends to a large extent on your level of mutual understanding with your shaper. He/she should therefore be deified, worshipped and applauded. Sadly, this seldom happens, and that is usually the shaper's fault. Shapers have many faults and you need to know the reasons why:

1   Shapers often let you down.

    Surfer I'm going overseas in two weeks' time. Can you make me two new boards by then?

    Shaper Sure, no problem.

    Surfer So you're not too busy. Because if you're too busy, I'll have to go somewhere else. I really need these boards.

    Shaper Like I said, no problem. Trust me.

2   Shapers make wild assumptions when in the process of shaping.

    Surfer But I asked for a swallow tail. This is a square tail.

    Shaper I've seen you surf and thought that you'd be better with a square tail.

    Surfer But this isn't the board that I ordered and paid for in advance.

    Shaper Just try it. It'll go like a bomb. Trust me.

3   Shapers are highly temperamental.

Shaper I heard you were surfing on some other shaper's board yesterday.

Surfer Erm, I was just having a go on it, trying out a different design.

Shaper Well, so much for loyalty then. In fact, so much for friendship as well.

Surfer But I ordered some boards two months ago and you never made them!

Shaper I would rather not ride any boards at all than turn my back on loyalty.

Surfer But I'm going away tomorrow and you still haven't made my boards!

Shaper Whatever, 'buddy'. You've obviously made your choice.

4   Shapers tend to forget that most boards these days are actually made by machines, and that all they do is twiddle a few knobs at the controls. But it has to be conceded that it's how, what and when they twiddle that can make the difference.

Shaper I slaved night and day with my broken back to make that board, and now you tell me you don't want it?

Surfer That board was machine-made in less than 20 minutes. What are you talking about?

Shaper Yes, but I made the machine by hand under extreme duress.

Surfer But it was flown in from a factory in Australia!

Shaper Are you calling me a liar? I made you the surfer that you are today, and this is how you thank me?

Should you have the opportunity to deal with a shaper, you will need to believe that they are, in general, perfectly acceptable people. Somehow, sometimes they manage to translate your surfing skills to the right board underfoot, and for that you have to be eternally grateful. Their strangeness and unreliability can probably be blamed on the fumes they breathe while working alongside the following board specialists.

GLASSERS, SANDERS AND SPRAYERS

The glasser's job is to seal the shaped foam 'blank' with fibreglass, keeping it light and strong. They also have to interpret the client's instructions on the order form to determine what sort of glassing has been requested. Rarely do they read the order form correctly. (It's something to do with the fumes.)

When the glasser has finished his job and the resin has set, the sander takes over and sets out to make the lump of heavy, rough resin into an aesthetically appealing piece of equipment. The biggest problem a sander faces is 'sanding through' (breaking through the resin to the foam core blank) which means the board will need to be repaired even before the client gets a chance to ride on it. This is not good. However, if a sander sands through, he can also use the fume excuse.

Then the spray artist comes into the equation. These days most surfers just want white boards, but occasionally a 1980s throwback decides that he wants a two-tone look with black-and-white checks, or a 1970s hippy decides that he wants a groovy, bare-breasted, life-sized mermaid on the bottom of his board that will 'allow him to communicate with the sea spirits, dude', and give off good karma while he surfs.

You should take careful note that people also refer to rails when discussing cocaine, so best not to ask for a rail in the wrong company.

If the mermaid isn't exactly what the client requested, the artist usually throws his hands in the air, shouts that no one understands him and his art, and resigns on the spot. These resignations are rarely spoken about because the artist merely returns to work the next day when the client isn't around and no one mentions a word about the resignation tantrum. But if they do, it's usually blamed on the fumes.

BOARD REFINEMENTS

Tail shapes

This refers to the end of the surfboard (the opposite end to the pointy bit) and there are three basic designs:

The square tail A tail that is squared off and provides bite for 'dynamic direction' changes. Very popular among those who surf mainly gentle ripples.

The round tail A tail that is rounded off, usually favoured by surfers who prefer bigger waves and less dynamic direction changes. Not to be confused with J.Lo's tail.

The swallow tail A tail with a shape that resembles a swallow. Imagine a squared-off tail with an inverted 'V' cut into it. An all-rounder that works for both big and small waves.

Most surfers can't really tell the difference between their tails while riding, but bluffers will be obliged to know what the tail shapes are meant to do.

Rails

These are the edges of the surfboards and the bits that bite into the water when turning. They can be either hard-edged or soft. The softer edges are more forgiving and enable surfers not to fall off so much while turning. Older surfers, longboarders, bluffers and surfers with little or no skill like softer edges best. Hard rails are found on performance boards preferred by small wave rippers and competitive surfers who want to get the most out of their waves and turns. You should take careful note that people also refer to rails when discussing cocaine, so best not to ask for a rail in the wrong company.

Rocker

This is the amount of curve the board has – the mild banana shape that prevents the board from digging in or nose-diving when paddling for a wave.

The basic premise is that the more rocker or curve a board has, the less chance of nose-diving. However, more rocker also means the board will travel more slowly across the water. So, short of a master's degree in hydrodynamics, the shaper's (or shaping machine's) skill lies in giving the board enough rocker to prevent nose-diving, while leaving it flat enough to hold a modicum of momentum. Simple, really.

Bottom shapes

The bottom of your board also affects the way it rides, and the variation in bottom shapes is not just limitless but in constant development. Concaves under the board, which provide lift and thus speed, may therefore give way to channel bottoms, bottoms with 'vee' (unsurprisingly, V-shaped bottoms), flat bottoms or textured bottoms.

Bluffers may wish to avoid conversations involving bottom shapes since most encourage sexual innuendo. This is below the status of surfers who are universally recognised as sexual sophisticates who are above such infantile behaviour.

Fins

There are two main fin set-ups: glassed-on fins and removable fins. The glassed-on kind are advisable because, being integral, there is hardly any drag, which means increased speed. The removable fins are advisable because when you are travelling, they eliminate the wasted space that boards with fins take up when placed together in a cover. It's also easier to replace removable fins with bigger fins or fins with more flex to see if the board moves better. A board that feels terrible the first time you ride it can come alive when you try new fins on it.

Removable fins are also surprisingly versatile on the beach. They can be used:

- as bases in baseball or goal posts in football

- to open beers

- to dig your vehicle out of the sand

- to wave at desirable members of the opposite sex

- as plates for sandwiches

- as rudimentary knives for buttering bread on camping trips

- to terrify swimmers by pretending to be a shark

- should the need arise, for digging holes in the sand to bury your dog's turds.

GET THE LOOK

What to wear is just as important as your choice of board, so the bluffer should start with the most essential bit of kit:

WETSUITS

The invention of wetsuits is generally accredited to Jack O'Neill, a surfer from Santa Cruz in California, although twins Bill and Bob Meistrell from Redondo Beach and Hugh Bradner from La Jolla (both also Californians) would beg to differ. It's a long-standing dispute but as long as surfers are kept warm, who really cares?

Wetsuits do not keep you dry (hence the name). They allow a little bit of water to seep in, which sits between your naked skin and the neoprene inside layer of the wetsuit. Your body temperature then heats this water, which keeps you warm. Thus a wetsuit's effectiveness is actually measured by the amount of heated water that it doesn't allow back out.

An easy way of warming up the water inside your

wetsuit is by urinating in it immediately. Every surfer, man or woman, does this, but it is rarely spoken about. If the world were to know that surfers actually ride waves sheathed in a suit filled with their own urine, their coolness quotient might be somewhat compromised.

The wetsuit you choose depends on your body shape and the water you're going to surf in. They come in different thicknesses, measured in millimetres. A 5/4/3, for example, is a suit that has five, four and three millimetre sections (thicker 5mm sections are generally for the parts of the wetsuit that have the least movement, i.e., the chest). Wetsuits with 5mm sections are made for very cold conditions. Contrary to some wetsuit advertising campaigns, having a wetsuit on doesn't mean that it's always summer on the inside; it just means that your immersion in the surf is going to be tolerable as opposed to intolerable.

A full suit covers the whole body except the head, hands and feet. When the water is warmer, a 'Short John' is useful – a wetsuit with no arms and short legs. There also used to be a wetsuit called a 'Long John', doubtless named after the popular thermal underwear garment.

The wetsuit for women is cut slightly differently, for obvious reasons, and they're allowed to wear pretty, mixed colours. Men should stick to one colour, and avoid anything bright or patterned. In fact, you should claim knowledgeably that sea blue is the best colour of all because sharks can only see in black and white and thus will be less likely to see you. According to the US Navy, yellow is most likely to attract them, but mainly because of the high level of contrast – not the colour itself which, obviously, they won't be able to see.

LEASHES

Leashes are things that attach your feet to the board. They are a good idea because they help you to avoid:

- spending a long time under the water without oxygen

- having to go all the way to the beach to retrieve your board after a wipeout (a spectacular ejection into the waves)

- your board flying into the shallows and bashing innocent bathers over their heads.

The longer or thicker leashes are designed for big waves, and thus offer maximum bluffing potential. Even if you never have cause to use them, you can throw them casually on to the table in beach bars when you're sure someone is looking.

When you are competing in small waves, drag can become a bit of an issue, so a thin, short leash – the 'comp leash' – is the one to use. It provides little or no drag, which enables you to generate maximum speed. But when the waves are very big then drag is not an issue. You have more to worry about – such as staying alive.

Note that leashes have other possible uses:

- They're useful for walking the dog.

- They can attach your cooler box to your ankle when you're dozing on the beach.

- They can be cunningly rigged as trip wires if someone is passing whom you need to speak to (shapers, attractive young men and women, someone who has recently 'dropped into' your wave (*see* Glossary), etc.).

FASHION AND ACCESSORIES

Surf fashion has come a long way since the dreadful neon days of the 1980s, and while it may have changed, no one can be sure if it has all changed for the good. On the whole there are two types of surf fashion: the very right one and the very wrong one.

The right surf fashion excludes anything that isn't a genuine surf brand. As a rule of thumb, these are the ones that sponsor top surfers and big surf tournaments around the world, and advertise in all the hardcore surf magazines. Their products are carefully designed and engineered to keep you warm in the water, to make you look cool, and to make you appear attractive to the sex to which you are romantically inclined.

The surf industry model is simple. Manufacture products and items that surfers need or desire and then charge approximately a 17,000% markup. As a result of the products being so ridiculously overpriced as well as nice to look at, surfers will covet them, buy them and flaunt them. This is what you need to wear if you want to be cool. Get it right and it'll be the biggest boost in credibility that the bluffer can hope for.

On the other hand, there are large chain stores that sell their own surf products and fashion items. Because they have many hundreds of retail outlets they can sell products at a fraction of the price that the surf industry can. This is known as economy of scale; it is also known as fashion to avoid. It will make you look like a cheapskate – worse, it will make you look like a very incompetent bluffer, and you can't afford to take that risk.

The surf industry model is simple. Manufacture products and items that surfers need or desire and then charge approximately a 17,000% markup.

The unavoidable reality is that you're going to have to bite the bullet and invest in the real thing – however ruinously expensive it is. And don't imagine that you can pick up authentic surfing gear in second-hand shops. Surfers rarely part with their clothes. The older and more tattered it is, the cooler it looks. That's why so much surfing fashion is of the 'ready-distressed' variety. (And ready-distressed is what you'll be after paying a small fortune for a T-shirt.)

Surfing hats used to be uncool, but when surfers started losing their noses and ears to skin cancer (not a good look), they rapidly became very definitely cool.

Headbands and pirate-knotted 'kerchiefs are totally uncool and must never be worn.

If surfing in shark-infested waters, deterrents such as Shark Shield, an electrical wave apparatus which is supposed to cause uncomfortable spasms in a shark's snout, are expensive, cumbersome and as yet unproven. You will earn maximum bluffing points, however, for knowing that a shark has special sensing organs called electroreceptors in its snout, otherwise known as 'the ampullae of Lorenzini'. And they don't like anything that interferes with them, which means that they're likely to do one of two things: tear you limb from limb in a frenzy, or swim off in a hurry. The jury is still out on which option they're most likely to choose. While you're waiting for a verdict, you can always invest in a branded Shark Shield carry case and fill it full of beer. This is a reasonably sensible and cost-effective option.

Waterproof smartphone cases are uncool, as is a floating barbecue supported on inflatable rings for cooking at sea. Don't be fooled into using any of these items. Be strong. You now know what is cool and what isn't. And, as a general guide, anything that isn't strictly necessary is naff. The easiest way for a bluffer to determine what is vital from what is not is to evaluate accessories in terms of functionality. If the accessory has little real function then it's probably just an affectation, and bluffers should not be seen dead wearing or using it. The following are examples of accessories that are functional and therefore permissible:

1. Sunglasses An absolute necessity whatever the shape or size. It is important that they have good UV lenses and make you look cool. Mirrored lenses are simply unacceptable – and try to avoid anything with too garish a tint. They'll just make you look like an idiot. Elasticated straps are advisable because sunglasses always fly off in a fall. Try to get something faded and threadbare which makes you look like you've been around a lot.

2. Nose guards Not shields to keep the sun off your nose, but the protective rubber sheaths for the nose (sharp end) of your surfboard. These must be high on your shopping list to avoid getting a sharp piece of fibreglass in your eye while surfing. Instead, you'll get a blunt chunk of rubber in your eye – much better for you.

3. Wetsuit accessories For really cold water there are wetsuit accessories that are well worth considering, such as:

- **Rubber and nylon boots** to keep your feet warm (called 'booties', unsurprisingly)

- **Nylon or rubber hood** to keep your head warm in freezing conditions (known as a 'hoodie', unsurprisingly)

- **Rubber surfing gloves** to keep your hands warm while surfing (called gloves, not 'glovies', surprisingly).

4. Sunscreen This is a must. Controversy reigns regarding its ratings system but, generally speaking, an SPF (sun protection factor) of 15 means you can go into the sun for 15 times longer than normal before you start burning. Whatever level you choose, when the sun is beating down, slop on as much as you can. You might look a bit of a freak but you'll be thankful when you get older and still have a face that doesn't resemble an old leather handbag.

5. A book A useful way of underlining your bluffing credentials is to carry a well-thumbed copy of *Barbarian Days: A Surfing Life*, by *The New Yorker* writer William Finnegan. It has been described as a 'memoir of an obsession, a complex enchantment'. It is not necessary to actually read it, although it is recommended. But if you don't have the time all you need to know is that it is the ultimate handbook for surfing initiates, acknowledging the sport as 'a beautiful addiction, a morally dangerous pastime, a way of life'. If you didn't already know, it won the 2016 Pulitzer Prize, and is thus a vital accoutrement for bluffers – especially when folded open and used as a sun shield on your face. Don't leave home without it.

Other 'essential' items have come and gone, like headbands of the McEnroe/Borg kind, or dog tags of the sort worn by squaddies, or shark's teeth necklaces (now about as cool as wearing fur). A few unlikely contenders have managed to stay, such as wetsuits with built-in heaters which plug into a car battery.

There are also multi-functional waterproof watches that tell the tide, the phases of the moon, have built-in USB cables and storage memory, talk to you and remind you of meetings, have heat timers for the competitive surfer, hack into the Pentagon and, believe it or not, sometimes tell the time. Remember never to wear them in the water. Free spirits surf with as little junk as possible.

An increasing number of websites and apps are linked to cameras on beaches so that you can look at the waves to see if the conditions are worth a surf without actually going there. A smart device is a must-have for the bluffer who wants to look knowledgeable about changing surf conditions – even if he or she can't tell the difference between a tsunami and a ship's wake.

Need to know In his book *Barbarian Days*, William Finnegan recounts riding a huge wave at Honolua Bay, in Maui, while under the influence of LSD. That's the idea: make a terrifying experience even more terrifying by adding the helpful ingredient of a mind-expanding drug. Shake your head at the folly of youth, but with a wry and knowing smile.

Over the years, surfers have been deliberately dismissive of wave size in order to sound more macho or brave.

WAVE ESSENTIALS

Now that you know a thing or two about gear, the next most important thing to acquaint yourself with is waves. They're rather vital to the sport.

WAVE HEIGHT

Over the years, surfers have been deliberately dismissive of wave size in order to sound more macho or brave. So, when a huge wave crashes through a lineup (*see* Glossary) and sweeps everyone up, and breathless and terrified people all debate how big the wave was, the surfer who drawls laconically, 'I've seen bigger waves in my bathtub', is striking the right note – even more so if he or she was actually in the water when the wave arrived.

There are three ways of measuring waves: from the front, from behind and relative to yourself.

From the front

This is the most common way. It is a measurement of

the wave face, from trough to crest. And it gives plenty of scope to exaggerate wave heights.

From behind

This is a Hawaiian method. It has even more macho potential than measuring from the front. A wave coming out of deep water and heading for a shallow reef can be, for example, 10 feet from behind but can actually have a wave face of 25 feet. It is important to note at this point that surfers around the world have never embraced the metric system. In fact, they're probably in breach of every EU directive and should therefore be applauded for being one of the last bastions of the imperial measure. As a result, it would be utter folly to refer to a surfing-related measurement in metres and centimetres. This applies to wave size and board length alike.

Reef breaks have been known to break surfboards, arms, legs, leashes and spirits.

Relative to yourself

This is the best way and the one bluffers should use to stay in the game. It goes like this. If a wave is very small, it's 'knee-high'; a bit bigger and it's 'waist-high'; then it gets to 'shoulder-high', and bigger than that brings you to 'head-high'. The increments continue to 'overhead', 'double overhead' and 'triple overhead'. After this it goes into another realm of measurement reporting that bluffers will never have any need to use.

Need to know The biggest wave ever recorded was in Alaska's Lituya Bay in 1958 when a landslide of 30.6 million cubic metres of rock generated a wave 1,720 feet high. Five deaths were recorded, all unfortunate people in boats who must have had a spectacular view of a wall of water nearly a third of a mile high just before it hit them. The biggest wave ever surfed and recorded is currently thought to be at Nazaré in Portugal in 2013. *The Guinness Book of Records* has estimated its height at 78 feet, but contemporaneous accounts suggest that it was actually nearer a hundred. (*See* page 111).

TYPES OF WAVES

Waves are generally recognised by the surfaces over which they break. Here are the various types:

BEACH BREAKS

These are the most forgiving of waves and generally considered the safest. They are used by surfers who are nervous about rocks, surfers who often fall off their boards and older surfers. This is not to say that beach breaks don't ever produce serious waves. Sometimes the sand packs hard and in perfect triangular shapes, and the beach break waves get to be among the best in the world.

Beaches to rave about are Puerto Escondido in

Mexico; Noordhoek in Cape Town and North Beach in Durban, South Africa; Fistral in Cornwall, UK; and Manly in Australia. Because it is much softer to land on sand than on rock, beach breaks are also particularly popular with bluffers.

REEF BREAKS

These are made of rock or coral and have been known to break surfboards, arms, legs, leashes and spirits.

Often very shallow, these breaks are not advisable for beginners and are definitely out of bounds to bluffers. They are generally reserved for competent and experienced surfers and, due to their uniform shape, they are where surfers go to surf identical waves over and over again and really practise their moves, as well as determine the best places on the reef to catch the best waves.

Breaks with dangerous bottoms like these are intimidating. It is not easy to paddle your heart out for an eight-foot wave and look down at a reef that is barely covered in water, knowing that one mistake is going to take you into a whole new world of pain.

Some of the best waves in the world are reef breaks and include waves like Pipeline in Hawaii, Grajagan in Indonesia, Teahupoo in Tahiti and Aileen's and Mullaghmore Head in Ireland. If asked whether you have surfed any of them, gaze stoically into the distance, ruminatively squeeze your shoulder and say softly 'it's not easy to talk about'. This is true, of course, because you know absolutely nothing about it.

POINT BREAKS

These generally occur where there is a bend in the coast outwards or inwards, i.e., a bluff (no pun intended) or a bay, and the wave travels along the bend in a constantly uniform manner. Point breaks are the surfers' ideal because they tend to go very long distances without much deviation in shape, form or speed, allowing surfers to surf fluidly and stylishly. Jeffreys Bay in South Africa is probably the best point break in the world, and the Superbank on the Gold Coast of Australia is another.

Due to their excellent shape and form, point breaks can be:

- the ones that attract the most crowds

- the ones that generate the best talent

- the most violent of surf spots (*see* 'Surf rage' in the Glossary).

Bluffing note *Point Break* is a Hollywood surf movie starring Keanu Reeves, Patrick Swayze and Gary Busey (*see* page 96). Originally it was going to be called *Riders on the Storm* which would have been an arguably better title. Bluffers will need to know about this sort of thing and be able to quote freely from Swayze's character Bohdi, viz. *'Fear causes hesitation, and hesitation will cause your worst fears to come true.'* Nod meaningfully when you say this, but don't attempt to explain it.

SLABS

Slabs are usually large, flat rocks over which a swell surges and then peels off for a few metres on either side. They are the most dangerous type of wave because they are usually very shallow. They are also known by a number of other cheerful names such as 'blood reefs', 'slabs of death' and 'tombstones'.

Slabs have one unexpected function – to serve as the ideal studios for surf photographers; the adjacent deep water allows them to set up in boats and get really close to surfers flirting with death or serious injury over and over again.

WEDGES

Wedge waves are formed when a wave heading towards the beach is met by a wave that has refracted off a rock outcrop, a pier or a man-made construction that juts into the sea like a harbour wall. When the two waves join, they form a peak which is bigger than the two separate waves and combines the energy of both. Wedge waves also tend to break really close to the water's edge, making for great drama. For bluffers, wedges of the potato variety are a more sensible option.

ARTIFICIAL WAVES

Not the kind provided by amusement parks (but not much better), the Wave Loch or FlowRider shoots a thin film of water over a rubber ramp to form a shallow, stationary wave over six-feet tall. It was the brainchild of American surfer-inventor Tom Lochtefeld who has taken it to many landlocked parts of the world, and there is a growing number of the things in existence. Especially on cruise ships.

Broken bones are commonplace,
but are not as bad as shattered egos.

A bluffer could practise for days on a FlowRider to get the hang of surfing in an accelerated mode, but the problem is the wipeout. If you fall off your Flowboard the whole thing happens in close proximity to spectators drinking beer and laughing at you. Broken bones are commonplace, but are not as bad as shattered egos.

CRAZY WAVES

Nature makes water behave strangely – look no further than the tsunamis that follow earthquakes. Slightly less dramatic water phenomena provide two crazy waves for bluffers to drop into conversation:

The Severn bore, Bristol Channel, UK

'The Severn bore,' you will say casually, 'is an example of a self-reinforcing solitary wave or solution.' At certain combinations of tides, the rising tidal water is funnelled up the estuary into a wave that travels rapidly upstream against the river current. Though not in itself a very good wave, and usually occurring when the temperatures are freezing, it can be ridden for several miles. According to some sources, 'Severn' is derived from the name Sabrina – based on the mythical story of the drowning of a nymph in the river – but you wouldn't want to dwell on that too long. Take care when claiming to have ridden the Severn bore all the way from the Second Severn Crossing to Stourport-on-Severn. It doesn't go that far, and nobody in their right minds would attempt it anyway. It's far too cold and it will almost certainly be raining.

The Pororoca, Amazon River, Brazil

The Pororoca is a river bore on a much grander scale. The name comes from the indigenous Tupi language, and translates as 'great destructive noise'. The wave can be heard 30 minutes before it arrives, and it destroys things like trees and houses on the river's edge. It has been known to pick up casual, unsuspecting fishermen in their canoes and deposit them up to 20km upstream, in a place that resembles a shit creek minus paddles.

The longest recorded Pororoca wave surfed was 12.5km and took over 37 minutes to ride out. If you feel tempted to mention these facts at a dinner party, and find yourself confronted about why you have never ventured out to the Amazon jungle to ride this wave, there is one bit of vital information you can use to save face. The Amazon River is rife with penile parasites, and surfers who attempt to surf the Pororoca are advised to wear condoms at all times. Seeing as they are open to attack by similar parasites, female surfers would also need to take appropriate precautions. And then there are the piranhas. . .

LEARN TO FORECAST

It's all very well knowing the different sorts of waves, but you will be accorded much more respect if you actually know where they're breaking. So make full use of the various reports that arrive in your email inbox or on your wave app (sometimes for free and sometimes for a fee) to let you know when and where the waves are going to get good, and how good they are going to get. They're also ideal for organising sick days well in advance.

Assimilating this wealth of information takes time and effort, so here are some shortcuts to use when attempting to hoodwink other surfers with your swell-forecasting abilities:

1. Insist that whichever website you choose (e.g., magicseaweed.com, windguru.com, buoyweather. com) 'is far more accurate on long-term predictions and has never let me down'.

2. Comment on swell direction (very important when making a prediction). If you were to pronounce to a group of surfers that 'I don't think that the new swell is going to get into the bay because it has too much east on it', people will look at you with respect, regardless of what direction is actually needed. Swell direction is generally only discussed by the experts, so you'll rarely get exposed.

3. Take a guess at the swell period. It is the measurement of time taken from the crest of one wave until the crest of the next wave, with the longer period indicating a stronger swell. Anything with a period below 10 seconds is weak, above 10 seconds is strong, and if it approaches a period of 16 seconds it is a very powerful swell – e.g., 'The swell is east-south-east with a 14-second period so we're bound to get a few waves at the northern end of the bay.'

4. Memorise a few names of forecasters with whom to disagree about the predicted size of swell, and always reckon that it will be smaller. This way, people will think your forecast tools are spot on, or that you're a big-wave surfer who downsizes waves due to your cavalier approach to big-wave surfing. It doesn't matter what the waves are actually doing when the predicted swell arrives; what matters most is how quietly convincing you sound.

THE BIG BREAKERS

There is no better opportunity for some shameless bluffing than when discussing the biggest, scariest, gnarliest, most insanely suicidal waves around the world's oceans. These are the ones that genuine surfers, for whom survival is not a priority, joyfully plunge into. Naturally you'll be well acquainted with all of them (from the comfort of your armchair), including the notorious Mavericks in Santa Cruz, California – the subject of a big-budget Hollywood biopic about 16-year-old Jay Moriarity whose famous wipeout on the wave was caught on film and made the cover of *Surfing* magazine (*see* page 99). Drop some of the following waves into any surfing conversation, hint that you have ridden and survived them, and you will have the rapt attention of your audience for as long as it takes to put them off surfing for life.

1. BANZAI PIPELINE, HAWAII

Pipeline is one of the most terrifying waves in the world. More people have died surfing here than anywhere else. Someone dies at Pipeline every other year, which is a grim pearl of knowledge that you will insist made it impossible for you to resist the temptation to ride it. The best surfer ever to surf Pipeline is Gerry Lopez (still an American surfing legend at nearly 70) and the surfer who has won the most Pipeline Masters events is 11-time world champion Kelly Slater (*see* page 109). Both of them are still alive (at the time of writing).

Need to know When the surf gets to a certain size, then 'Second Reef Pipeline' starts breaking further out. It's actually slightly easier to catch a wave on the Second Reef and then ride it through First Reef on the inside. Don't worry about what this means; just remember to mention nonchalantly that you 'only surf when Second Reef is breaking'. Prepare for jaws to drop in admiration.

2. WAIMEA BAY, HAWAII

Another big-wave spot on the North Shore of Oahu, Waimea was for many years the big-wave epicentre of the world. In the good old days, surfers had to paddle into one of the most dangerous big waves around without the help of jet skis or inflatable wetsuits. Many people have lost their lives surfing here as well – a compelling reason for claiming that you have surfed it and survived. It is also home to the most prestigious big-wave surfing contest in the world, commonly known as 'The Eddie'.

Need to know The catchphrase when talking about the contest is 'The bay calls the day'. This a reference to wave height and whether or not The Eddie will go ahead. Express profound disappointment if it is cancelled, saying that surf is not what it used to be. Blame global warming.

3. JEFFREYS BAY, SOUTH AFRICA

One of the longest and most perfect waves in the world, Jeffreys Bay (also known as J-Bay) is also one of the most shark-infested. Naturally, you will say that this makes it even more of a challenge. Nearly all waves in South Africa have a resident great white called The Submarine (on account of its size) or The Destroyer (on account of its propensity to destroy). Jeffreys Bay also has some pushy local surfers called the Jeffreys Bay Underground or JBU. You'd be better off taking your chances with the sharks.

Need to know The most popular sections of the wave are called Boneyards, Supertubes and The Point, but there are also sections called Salad Bowls and Coins. Bluffers can always mention that they tend to stay away from the 'Hollywood stretches' and prefer to surf Salad Bowls and Coins, because that's where Slater hangs out.

4. DUNGEONS, SOUTH AFRICA

This is the biggest wave in South Africa and one of the biggest in the southern hemisphere. Bluffers should mention that they prefer to take off on the Two-Point-Four peak as opposed to the outside peak, as the wave breaks a bit harder in the shallow water. What this means is that the Two-Point-Four section breaks over 2.4 metres deep water, while the Outside breaks in very deep water.

Need to know There is another part of the wave called 'The Slab', but that's only for real nutters. Avoid it at all costs. And if you happen to be in the area, don't say that you hitched a lift with the Nauticat. That's the tourist boat that goes past the wave on its way to Seal Island. It's tempting, but it's not cool.

5. SNAPPER ROCKS, AUSTRALIA

The wave at Snapper Rocks on the Gold Coast in Australia is a modern phenomenon. There used to be a number of waves along that stretch of coastline, called Snapper Rocks, Greenmount, Rainbow Bay, Kirra and others, but when the local council started pumping sand from the mouth of the nearby Tweed River, the sand collected around the corner and formed one of the longest waves in the world, the Snapper Superbank. Boscombe, near Bournemouth in England, has tried to follow suit by building an artificial reef (but don't say you've surfed it – there's not much bluffing potential here).

Need to know The longest wave ridden at Snapper, you will point out knowledgeably, was by local surfer Damon Harvey and was reported to be over 1.5km long. It took about four minutes to ride, which is some going.

6. OURS, AUSTRALIA

Located at Cape Solander, Kurnell, near Sydney, the name of this reef break has an unusual and decidedly un-surflike-international-brotherhood-of-love-hate story behind it. The wave now known as Ours had been surfed happily by bodyboarders for a few years until local surfers from the nearby suburb of Maroubra discovered it and co-opted it as 'theirs'. They called it, imaginatively, 'Ours' and made it emphatically clear that no one else was welcome – especially bodyboarders (unless they wanted to get thumped). Nice going, guys!

Need to know Among the surfers from Maroubra is a surf gang called 'The Bra Boys' (nothing apparently to do with cross-dressing, but more of a reference to the last syllable of Maroubra) and their story was made into an award-winning documentary of the same name. Before the recent fuss, Ours was known as Pikers Hole – which some might say is a much better name.

7. SHIPSTERN BLUFF, AUSTRALIA

This ferocious right-hander is tailor-made for bluffers, not just because it's the only big wave with the word 'Bluff' actually in its name but because so few people have surfed it. Down at the bottom of Tasmania and also known as 'The Wave at the End of the World', Shipstern Bluff must rank with Pipeline as one of the scariest waves on the planet. Take a look at *As Big As It Gets* on YouTube, and if that terrifying chasing wall of water doesn't have your bowels turning to even more water than usual, then you are a man of steel (otherwise known as a robot, not known for their swimming ability). Churned up by the Roaring Forties, this is as cold, gnarly and isolated as surfing gets – which is why all bluffers must claim to have been there. Very few could possibly dispute this, because they won't have been there, either.

Need to know Getting to Shipstern involves a long bushwalk from the only road (or a boat ride from Hobart for the wealthy) and there are very few signposts to point you in the right direction. The locals tend to rip them up. *Tracks* magazine first made the wave famous with a memorable photoshoot, but it was reluctant to expose the exact location and named it 'Fluffytonka' in the article. (Further bluffing points can be earned for knowing that it was once called Devil's Point – for a very good reason.)

8. ULUWATU, BALI

Prettily located on the Bukit peninsula of Bali in Indonesia, Uluwatu is now a less-than-inviting place to go and visit. There can be hundreds of surfers in the water, no real system in the lineup, increasing pollution and dangerous coral. All in all it's not one of those desperate-to-surf-before-you-die destinations. The waves are great, however, and it is one of the most beautiful surf destinations in the world. With some of the most beautiful people.

Need to know The local Indonesian ladies offer all sorts of magical massages and treatments on the beach after a long session in the surf – probably the best available anywhere in the surf world. Maybe you don't need to know this.

9. G-LAND, JAVA

Grajagan, or G-Land, is a jungle surf camp located in Java, Indonesia. American Bob Laverty discovered it in 1972, spotting it from a plane, and discovered what was known for many years as the best left-breaking wave in the world. Bob set up a rudimentary treehouse camp for surfers which allowed even the most financially challenged to ride G-Land. Surfers and bluffers everywhere should be grateful to him. In 1994 a tsunami tore through the jungle camp at night, carrying some very well-known surfers hundreds of metres into the jungle, but no one was killed. It's not a good idea to claim to have been there and to have survived by successfully riding the wave.

Need to know While everyone talks about the four main sections of the wave, being Kongs, Moneytrees, Launchpads and Speed Reef, bluffers can also mention 'The Cobra' – a rare section of the wave that comes to life on certain swells and certain tides.

10. RIFLES, SUMATRA

This is a rare beast located in the Playgrounds area of the Mentawai Islands, which sit about 100km west of

Sumatra, Indonesia. A long and perfect barrelling right-hand wave, Rifles is the Holy Grail of Indonesian surf Meccas (excuse the mix of religious metaphors).

Need to know The word 'rare' is employed here for a very good reason; some surfers have been to the area more than a dozen times and have yet to attain perfect surf conditions. Bluffers should also note that there is another wave around the corner called Pistols that also scores pretty well.

11. PASTA POINT, MALDIVES

An Australian named Tony Hinde discovered this surf spot and never left (as is often the case with Australians). Knowing a good thing when he chanced on it, he married a local girl and set up an exclusive surf camp tailored to the richer, older surfer. Clever guy. Surfing at Pasta Point is usually year-round and only allows 30 surfers at any one time.

Need to know Crucial bluffing info is that you can't surf at Pasta Point when the 'sweep' – a powerful current rushing between the atolls – kicks in. The sweep is also known as the Malé Express, named after the capital, and it will wash you very quickly out into the shipping lanes – where you really don't want to be on a board.

12. TAMARIN BAY, MAURITIUS

For many years, Tamarin Bay has been the crown

jewel of surfing in Mauritius. Not that it has a great deal of competition, seeing as the surf in Mauritius is rarely consistent and breaks very far out to sea beyond the coral lagoons. But when Tamarin Bay gets good, everyone in Mauritius who surfs heads there. That's not so good. While it might be a near-perfect wave, the locals argue that they should have preference when it breaks.

Need to know A gang of local surfers called the White Shorts guards this fickle wave fiercely. The members are pretty ruthless and dish out summary justice to surfers they don't like. Bluffers would be well-advised not to wear white shorts when surfing here.

13. ST LEU, RÉUNION ISLAND

This is the friendlier Indian Ocean surfing neighbour to Mauritius. Réunion has many good waves on it, the best known being St Leu, a perfect left-breaking wave that sits in the shadow of a volcano. However, St Leu gets very crowded and tense, with local surfers aggressively dominating the always-crowded lineup.

Need to know For many years, surfers could camp right on the point in front of the wave, and there was a well-known local surfer called Tarzan. Bluffers might legitimately say that they hung out with Tarzan who lived among the trees – when he wasn't in the water.

14. MAVERICKS, CALIFORNIA, US

Mavericks is an infamous surfing spot about a mile or more off Half Moon Bay, about 25 miles south of San Francisco in California. Waves regularly top 60 feet, and it has become one of the go to destinations for big-wave surfers in North America. Although it is known as a globally recognised invitational surf contest, it is more widely known for the deaths of champion surfers Mark Foo and Sion Milosky, and the 2012 film *Chasing Mavericks* (*see* page 99).

Need to know Mavericks owes its extreme nature to an unusual rock formation on the seabed, and owes its name to a white German Shepherd, Maverick, who regularly accompanied his surfing owner to the beach in the late 1960s.

You can be reasonably confident that whoever you're attempting to impress won't have been within half a continent's proximity of Skeleton Bay, Namibia.

---

15. SKELETON BAY, NAMIBIA

Skeleton (you might speculate with interest on how it got its name) is a brutal, bone-breaking breaker found in Namibia. It is a perfect bluffer's destination because very few people know how to get there, where to stay, how to organise a driver and what conditions make it worth the trip. In other words, you can be reasonably confident that whoever you're attempting to impress with your knowledge and experience won't have been within half a continent's proximity of it. Always say that it's a difficult place to score, but if you get it good, it could be the best surf of your life.

Need to know Bluffers can talk about other waves in the area like Cape Cross and Lockjoint, as well as the fine Namibian beer available from every guy with a cool box.

16. PUERTO ESCONDIDO, MEXICO

Sometimes known as the Mexican Pipeline, this is a huge beach break wave that gets very powerful and dangerous, and is thus irresistible to big-wave surfers. It should therefore be 'irresistible' to you. Bluffers should note that because the waves break so close to the shore, surfers do not attach their boards to their ankles with leashes, preferring to let the boards go and to wade back to retrieve them. This doesn't really happen anywhere else in the world.

Need to know Simply say: 'I just took my two eight-footers and no leashes to Escondido.' If your audience knows anything about surfing, they'll know what you're talking about. Oh, and don't forget to mention the lethal rip tides.

17. MUNDAKA, SPAIN

A perfect left-hand breaking wave in northern Spain (actually in the Basque country), it gets crowded and big, and is not for the faint-hearted. The wave breaks into the mouth of the Oka River, which runs through the town of Mundaka, and used to be the location of a World Tour surf event, the Billabong Pro Mundaka. However, this was cancelled because whenever they had a waiting period for the contest, the ocean would go flat and remain so until the pros had left town. Then, suddenly, a perfect, 10-foot wave would roll in consistently for days on end.

Need to know All you need to say is that Mundaka 'works best on a north swell and a south wind, which is actually quite rare'. You might also point out that the town is on the Bay of Biscay, which is one of the most turbulent large bodies of water in the world.

18. CLOUDBREAK, FIJI

The wave is about a mile from Tavarua Island, and you'll need a boat or a tow to get there. It was once reserved exclusively for well-heeled surfers who could afford to stay on the US-owned island resort. Even Fijian surfers born and bred in the area were not allowed to surf the wave unless they paid through the nose. One day not too long ago, the Fijian government changed all that and opened the wave up to the world. Bluffers armed with this knowledge could easily start an argument on the 'pay-to-surf' ideology and the pros and cons of exclusive waves and controlling access to them.

Need to know There are three main sections to Cloudbreak: the point (also called 'the top'), the middle, and the inside (called 'Shish Kebabs' because the shallow reef there can skewer you).

19. TEAHUPOO, TAHITI

Most of the literature on this wave has focused on how to pronounce its name. 'Cow-pooh', 'Tee-ah-hu-poo', 'Tea-hoo-poo', 'Chow-pooh' or 'Chuppie' are all popular contenders. The correct pronunciation is 'Cho-pooh', with 'Cho' pronounced the same as in the first syllable of 'chota peg' which is Anglo-Indian slang for a nip of spirits. Which doesn't really help at all. Anyway, a bluffer will show serious cred by calling it 'Chopes' and sticking to 'Chopes' no matter what anyone else says. Those in the know call it nothing else.

Need to know Chopes is dangerous and far from user-friendly. The little village in front of the wave is known as 'The End of the Road'.

20. BUNDORAN PEAK, IRELAND

This reef wave breaks left and right and is situated in County Donegal on the north-west coast of Ireland. It is cold and fickle and is only surfed by the hardy, strong, determined, dedicated, demented…well, you get the picture. 'The Peak' is one of the best waves in Europe and is not for the faint-hearted. Powered by Atlantic rollers, it's perilously close to some big rocks – no place to be when you take a dive.

Need to know There is a new big-wave spot just around the corner called Mullaghmore, where Lord Mountbatten was assassinated in 1979. William Butler Yeats is also buried nearby. And the stout in this part of Ireland is remarkably good.

SURFING TYPES

Surfers are classified by the type of boards they ride, the type of waves they prefer, or a combination of both. The enterprising bluffer will take a few pointers from the following:

THE SHORTBOARDER

This is the young, fit and fashionable surfer who can ride the thin, light and short boards without fear of their weight causing them to sink...

The shortboarder represents the biggest slice of the surfer demographic and thus composes about 90% of the crowds in the water. The most popular pro-surfing tours are aimed at shortboarders, although there are definitely professional surfers on tour who haven't seen their abs in a good while.

As soon as surfers get to a certain age, normally around the mid-30s when their chests start heading south, they must adapt if they wish to carry on surfing. This is the dreaded stage of having to give up the sport altogether and heading into a bar to bore everybody rigid about how you could have been a contender on the pro tour, or changing your equipment to the longboard which might just extend your surfing life.

Bluffers need to be seen as much as possible with or around shortboards or shortboarders. They are the coolest and most hip surfers around. They have good hair, wear the right gear and most of them can surf.

THE LONGBOARDER

Longboarders are generally treated as eccentrics. Their boards, which are throwbacks to the 1960s, are nine feet long, bulky, unwieldy and dangerous. Under the feet of older, unskilled surfers, the longboard is cruelly referred to as a 'barge', an 'unguided missile' or a 'plane wing'.

Longboarders are often so out of shape that they have to hire young kids to carry their plane wings from the water's edge to their cars, and then help them out of their wetsuits.

Despite these disparaging terms, the longboard has the distinct advantage of being a much faster paddler than the shortboard, which means the longboarder can often jump the queue and sneak waves off the shortboarder. This usually results in a few more interesting names for longboarders, generally involving human reproductive organs. Many longboarders understand the rules of wave sharing, though, and thus feel quite bad when they steal them from shortboarders. (Or so they claim.)

Longboarders are often so out of shape that they have to hire young kids to carry their plane wings from the water's edge to their cars, and then help them out of their wetsuits.

It is important for a bluffer to deny:

- owning a longboard

- being friendly with a longboarder

- yearning for yesteryear, when surfing was 'all about the soul and the glide'.

There are three subspecies of longboarder:

1. Original surfers who gave up surfing 20 years ago in the interest of focusing on career and family. Once they have more time on their hands, they return to the water with a longboard because it's the one they know. Bluffers should watch out. These longboarders have missed out on 20 years of surfing rules and etiquette, and all they want to do now is to catch up on all the waves they missed.

2. Novices who get a longboard to learn on because it is the easiest. They find themselves in the middle of a

system and pecking order without a clue as to what's going on, and will proceed at full speed completely unaware of the trail of destruction, fear and loathing that they leave behind.

3. Surfers who have been at it for years and years and just want to have fun. These are the ones who know all the rules and obey them. This makes their choice of equipment irrelevant because their fun is not going to spoil anyone else's.

THE RETRO SURFER

Sometimes also called the retrosexual, this is a species that arose out of the somewhat disdainful attitude towards the longboarder. Their choice is a shortboard, but one with a design from the 1960s or 1970s and usually thick and wide, which means the retro surfer can catch waves a lot easier than the shortboarder but without the stigma attached to the longboarder (subspecies one and two). The retro surfer also frequently sports a stomach of immense proportions and will therefore have no problems staying afloat.

The retro surfboard, you will declare, may well appear simple and stubby to the untrained eye but is actually a highly complex wave-riding vehicle. Paddling out to catch the waves is easy enough, but once up and riding, it requires a great deal of skill.

The Fish is the most popular retro surfboard, a twin-fin model originally designed by legendary American shaper Steve Lis. Other well-known retro boards are the quad-fin and the Bonzer, which was invented by the Australian Campbell brothers in 1970. As soon as they invented it, the brothers gave it all up and devoted their energy to starting a very successful restaurant business.

THE COMPETITIVE SURFER

This is a surfer with one thing in mind: doing as many turns on a wave as possible to get points for prizes.

The competitive surfer will cheat, rob, lie, cry, shout and sabotage if he or she believes it will help to win a heat.

Successful competitive surfers earn a lot of money from prizes and endorsements, and get their photos in magazines, which helps them get lucky. Sadly, many seem not to be enjoying themselves as much as they might. Instead of being a magic carpet ride, surfing becomes more of a tedious practice session for the next event.

THE FREE SURFER
(aka 'hippy' or 'soul surfer')

Free surfers surf purely for the love of the sport and, despite being some of the best surfers in the world, choose to turn away from its competitive side. They believe more in the ideology of surfing as a lifestyle or religion than as a sport, and dislike all forms of commercialism. Some free surfers get paid not insignificant amounts of money to espouse these beliefs.

Free surfers are able to choose whatever equipment they want since they don't need the most efficient boards to win trophies. Many choose retro boards (although none of them choose longboards).

They are keen on tofu and lentils, usually bearded (if male), practise yoga, knit their own muesli, wear black wetsuits and use white boards. Colour is the friend of the competitive surfer and the enemy of the free surfer. Free surfers do not cut their hair because, as Danny the drug dealer in the movie *Withnail and I* said, 'Hairs are your aerials. They pick up signals from the cosmos, and transmit them directly into the brain. This is the reason bald-headed men are uptight.' Free surfers believe stuff like this.

THE MOTORISED SURFER

With the introduction of the jet ski into the surfing realm, this type of surfer is the newest addition to the family. Many surfers, particularly soul surfers, emphatically reject them, complaining of noise pollution, fuel discharge in the water, danger to living creatures and danger to other surfers, while silently wishing that they could afford one.

Maritime law strictly controls the use of jet skis, and jet-ski drivers are required to pass competency tests and put stickers on their craft to say so. Unhappily, many jet-ski operators have never surfed before, and know little about waves.

The craft's principal use is to tow surfers into big and unruly waves, which would be effectively unsurfable on a normal paddle surfboard, when surfers using arm strength alone cannot get enough momentum to catch the wave. With the help of a jet ski, a surfer can quickly match the wave's speed and get towed into it, no matter how big it is. This is a matter of particular consternation to the big-wave soul-surfer who denounces the machine age, and sees the actual paddle as part of the challenge. Many personal water craft (PWC) ruling bodies have a regulation stating that if a paddle surfer is surfing a wave, jet skis are not allowed within a given distance of him or her (up to 300 metres). As more and more surfers are embracing the machine age in their once pure and unviolated sport, the authorities devise more cunning rules and restrictions to make it more difficult for them to enjoy it.

Bluffers should be aware that there is a particularly unpopular example of the motorised type of surfer. This is the one who is towed by the jet ski directly into comparatively small waves. Genuine surfers will know that the worst aspect of surfing ripples is the absence of wave energy, and thus the absence of speed. The little wave surfer on tow is given speed from his artificial propulsion. Some people think this is downright dishonest. Bluffers should publicly take the line that this sort of surfer should take up water skiing or kite surfing (*see* Glossary). On the other hand, it's a big ocean and there should be room for everyone – not least bluffers, who want to get the feeling of being swept along by a wave, and really don't want to find themselves out of their depth.

THE BIG-WAVE SURFER

The big-wave surfer is a surfer who is attracted, sometimes recklessly, to the biggest waves that the ocean can churn up. Big-wave surfers believe themselves to be the godhead of all surfers, and so they should. Their exploits in the giant waves of Waimea, Mavericks, Dungeons, Jaws, Teahupoo and Shipstern's can and do lead to premature departures from this life. Famous big-wave surfers who have drowned while surfing include Mark Foo, the Hawaiian surfer who perished at Mavericks in 1994 (*idem*); Todd Chesser, who was killed at Outside Alligators in Hawaii; Donnie Solomon, who was killed at crowded Waimea; and Malik Joyeaux, who drowned at Pipeline.

The surfers who live to surf monstrous waves are fully aware that the world at large knows they are crazy with a capital 'C'. To give themselves credibility they often indulge in forced bravado, spouting nonsense like, 'Fear is my friend', 'You have nothing to fear but fear itself', 'The worst thing that can happen is that you might die', or, to borrow Patrick Swayze's line in the movie *Point Break* – 'Shit happens.'

Big-wave surfing is unsurprisingly extremely dangerous territory for bluffers. If you ever get your bluff called on a day when the waves are particularly large, there are a few foolproof ways to bluff your way out of dangerous surf with your credibility still intact. These include 'I left my big-wave board behind', 'I've got a bad case of lumbago and can't risk it', 'My old Iraq war wound is playing up,' or the more aggressive,

'Just not big enough yet; I'm going to come back at lunchtime when it should be a bit bigger,' or 'Tide's too high; I'm going to come back at low tide when the rocks are actually sticking out of the water.' Tremulously whispering the words 'I'd be out there if I wasn't so scared witless' is never advisable.

THE STAND-UP PADDLEBOARDER (SUP)

The stand-up paddleboarder stands on a large surfboard and uses a paddle to catch a wave. It's a core workout and these surfers can catch waves easier than longboarders. SUP is very, very difficult to learn: even surfers who have been at the sport for over 20 years can struggle. Bluffers are advised not to try for SUPerman status of this sort, however tempting it might be to emulate the zen-like calm of a skilled practitioner.

THE ENEMY

The surfer does not have many enemies, but there are a few subspecies of the genus that are really difficult to tolerate.

The kneeboarder

Surfers always feel uneasy around people who kneel down on their boards, and always sing the Bob Marley number, 'Get Up, Stand Up' to the kneeler in a bid to humiliate them and get them to join the surfing brotherhood. The kneeboarder is usually a complex person, with a fair number of issues.

The bodyboarder
The bodyboarder lies supine on a square piece of sponge that passes for a board, and which is usually found in the supermarket aisle next to the water wings. With nicknames such as 'teabags', 'speed bumps', 'boogers' and 'doormats', there is little love lost between surfers and bodyboarders.

The paddle skier
This bizarre species flourished for a while and then disappeared, though it is rumoured that a few pockets still exist in remote corners of the world. Known as 'goat-boaters' or 'das booters', they are ridiculed for their craft of choice, a small wave-riding kayak, and the fact that they have to shift their weight from buttock to buttock in order to turn their craft on a wave.

PRO-SURFER GROUPIES

As with any sport that attracts massive amounts of sponsorship money, the top names have groupies hanging around holding placards with quaint slogans like 'KSKP' (Kelly Slater in my Knickers Please). They are mostly, but not exclusively, of the female persuasion.

Some surf groupies only come to life when the pro-surf tour lurches into their hometown; others, a bit more fanatical, will follow the tour around the world at their own expense. There are plenty of pro-surfer groupies and a smattering of surf photographer groupies. Surf journalist groupies are mystifyingly small in number.

Groupies save their cash for one huge month in Hawaii when all the pro surfers in the world are gathered in a small seven-mile stretch of the North Shore. Ravenous packs of groupies can be seen prowling the beaches looking for the pros. This could be a bluffer's heaven (if transient, meaningless, and loveless sexual gratification is your sort of thing). With the knowledge gleaned from this book, you will now be able to fool any groupie into believing that you are one of the top 20 surfers in the world. Most groupies are only *au fait* with the very top echelons of the tour, so if you aim a little further down the rung (say, number 19), you'll be able to fill your surf boots.

SURF WIDOWS

Surfers have the attitude that there might not be any waves the next day, or even the next hour, so it's important to surf when conditions are at their best. This often means an early surf run in the pre-dawn hours, leaving a spouse warmly tucked up in bed, or chasing a swell up the coast for a week or more at a moment's notice.

It can mean rushing out of your own wedding to surf the reef at high tide; or leaving the hospital and the arrival of your first child because the wind has just swung and the beach break might be getting good. It might mean a quick exit from the funeral of a family member, or even non-attendance if a brand new swell has arrived unexpectedly.

On rare occasions, it could result in your absence from your own birthday bash that your wife and family have set up for months and flown family in from all over the world to attend. If a good swell arrives, the dedicated surfer can become a tiny bit self-indulgent at times.

———————— *ß* ————————

If pressed for details, fall back on the usual modest shake of the head and reluctance to talk about anything to do with your glittering competitive record. You might mention that if it hadn't been for 'that' infamous wipe out at Nazaré, things might have been a lot different.

PRO SURFING

Competitive surfing can be credited with having grown the sport and enhanced its appeal. It has led to progress in riding techniques and board design, and has been largely responsible for popularising big-wave surfing in some of the world's most exotic locations. Every bluffer needs to be able to claim that they've been there and done it (how they had a famous surfer on the ropes for an entire heat before losing at the last second, or how they were placed in the top 10 of a surfing tour at some stage in their lives). Serious surfers need to have a competition pedigree for credibility, and bluffers will know all about the importance of credibility.

It is essential, therefore, that you should have more than a passing knowledge of professional surfing and what makes up the tour. Anybody worth their bluffing salt should be able to show disdain for the judges, scoff at the system and hint at a deeper understanding of how the sport works. Even, and this is the important part, if it's just so that you can say: 'Of course, I never really believed in competition surfing. Free surfing has always been my first love.'

THE WORLD SURF LEAGUE (WSL)

Professional surfing – not just a bunch of guys and girls frolicking happily in the surf – actually has a governing body that enables surfers to enter competitions, and then exacts exorbitant entrance fees and prize taxes from them in exchange for tacky trophies and a much-coveted place in the world rankings. It is known as **The World Surf League** and was previously known as the **Association of Surfing Professionals (ASP)** from 1983 to 2014. Bluffers are not really required to know much more than this about who controls competitive surfing, or anything about the tedious politics involved in the WSL's history (or future). But as with any other governing body, it is perfectly acceptable – in fact almost obligatory – to hold it in disdain and claim that it doesn't know what it's doing. If you happen to come across a surfer who sings the WSL's praises, then he or she will almost certainly be on their payroll. A useful lesson to bear in mind here is not to wade in with the usual contemptuous snort about general corporate incompetence, but to probe gently about the chances of getting a job on the tour. It is likely to be well paid, with a very generous expense account.

ISA (OLYMPICS)

There is another governing body known as the **International Surfing Association (ISA)** which organises competitions that have no money prizes but are simply about the glory. It has 103 member nations including firmly land-locked Afghanistan, Slovakia, and Switzerland. Bluffers should know that the ISA was behind a successful bid to have surfing included as a new sport at the 2020 Summer Olympics in Japan. The contest will be of the shortboard variety, for both men and women, and held on Shidashita Beach, in Chiba, 40 miles from Tokyo. Applications for ISA jobs have soared into the stratosphere.

SURF COMPETITIONS

Again you will not need to know a great deal about world championship surfing, for the very simple reason that you won't be participating in anything which is likely to strip away your pretence of expertise. You will hint, of course, at past triumphs and feats of valour. But if pressed for details, fall back on the usual modest shake of the head and reluctance to talk about anything to do with your glittering competitive record. You might mention that if it hadn't been for 'that' infamous wipeout at Nazaré, things might have been a lot different. If pressed for further details, walk away, accentuating a previously non-existent limp and say over your shoulder 'There's never any point in dwelling on the past and wondering what might have been.'

Bluffers are advised not to be over-ambitious when claiming a particular level of achievement in competition. Your best bet is to say that you fought your way through the QS (Qualifying Series) but became disenchanted with the 'circus'. There are so many aspiring champions competing at this level that it will be impossible to call your bluff. If you want to push your luck, claim that you made it to the CT (the holy grail of pro surfing) but as a 'wildcard' called in at the last minute. Again, this will be hard to dispute.

THE TOUR

The pro surfing tour is a world of constantly changing acronyms, slightly different acronyms, sometimes former acronyms, and no doubt future acronyms all guaranteed to create maximum confusion, but then that's what governing bodies exist for – to complicate things to ensure that senior officers are kept in post to explain how it all works. Prepare yourself for a wave of WTs, CTs, WSLs, ASPs, WCTs, WQSs, ISAs, and presumably some more currently in development.

Competition pro-surfing is divided into two tiers:

- the QS – Qualifying Series, formerly known as the WQS (World Qualifying Series)

- the CT – Championship Tour, formerly known as the WT (World Tour) or WCT (World Championship Tour).

Competitors in both are some of the luckiest people in the world, as they get paid incredible amounts of money to mess around in waves all over the globe. The main difference is that on the CT:

- the waves are generally much better

- the prize money is better

- the food is better

- the accommodation is better.

The QS is the stepping stone to the CT and every hopeful professional surfer has to qualify on the QS to make it onto the CT. The QS is commonly known as 'The Grind' due to the unremitting hardship and toil endured by contestants. It's tough having to surf for a living – getting paid to ride perfect waves at idyllic beaches the world over, usually in front of beautiful young men and women in various stages of undress.

The CT rankings determine the world champions and the QS rankings help determine who will be taking part in the CT in the following year.

The WSL coordinates the CT, the QS, the Big Wave Tour, the Longboard Championship, the Junior Championship, and the Masters Championship. Oddly the latter events are not known as the BWT, LC, JC, and MC. (Not yet, anyway.)

The overall WSL World Championship is won by any of the WSL's top 34 men's surfers, or the top 17 women's surfers who qualified to compete in the CT. The men and women surfers with the most points at the end of the CT year become the world champions.

The WSL top 34 men surfers comprise: the top 22 finishers on the CT rankings; the top 10 from the QS rankings; and two WSL Wildcards (these are surfers who wouldn't have otherwise qualified). Usually these are CT participants who were injured in the previous season and therefore unable to re-qualify. Note that there are event wildcards as well as WSL Wildcards. And then of course there are replacement surfers chosen to fill empty spots at CT events should any of the competitors be unable to compete. Quite clear on this?

The WSL top 17 women surfers are comprised of: the top 10 finishers on the CT rankings; the top 6 from the QS rankings; and one WSL Wildcard.

THE CT

The CT, as you will know now to call it, is an elite tour with events held at locations where the waves are more or less guaranteed to be good. It's also known as the 'Dream Tour' because it focuses more on the quality of waves than the number of bums on seats. This is a dream for those surfers who have tolerated years of awful surfing conditions to appease sponsors and make the grade.

The CT has held glorious events off the jungles of Java and at reef passes in Tahiti, where spectators have no place to spectate except from little boats in the channel. These are prime examples of events being held in the best waves possible so that the surfers get the most out of the contest, and not the spectators. The interests of the athletes are placed ahead of the spectator. Whoever would have thought it?

If you make it onto the CT, you can go home and tell your father, 'Dad, I made it.' The big trick, once you've made it onto the CT, is to stay on it. The CT is such a different place from the QS that it is possible to use the system to remain there for a number of years, earning good money and enjoying all the perks of being a top surfer.

THE QS

'The Grind' is a kind of free-for-all for aspiring surfers the world over. It is known as The Grind for a very good reason. It's a long, hard slog for most surfers to get all the way to the CT. There are thousands of QS surfers and hundreds of events the world over – most of them taking place in not very good waves.

QS events are graded on a star system. Simply put, the higher the star rating, the more points and prize money available for that event. So the goal is to surf the highest-rated events and do well in them. Well, that's the objective. But with thousands wanting to achieve it and only a few who will do so, it can get a bit desperate. Plenty of distractions, and the thrill of travelling to new countries and exploring new cultures and cuisines, are reckoned to be enough to quell any negative thoughts if you haven't done too well. It's a lot better than surfing around the world by waiting tables.

Grind parties are prime hang-outs for bluffers – and even better if you can get hold of a competitor's bracelet. These admit surfers into clubs and bars for free and accord them special service from bar and restaurant staff. They also indicate to prospective sexual partners that you are a free-spirited, hard core competitive surfer.

As a first step, you need to bluff your way on to a 'contest tower' and secure a media bracelet. The best way to do this is to say that you're a reporter working for one of the big newspapers or magazines and want to interview a few interesting people. If this doesn't work, you could try to bribe the security guard who controls admission to the tower. A last resort would be to present an official-looking business card for a fictitious new surf magazine and say that this contest report is going to be in the first issue. Otherwise, you can always try getting on your knees and grovelling pathetically.

Once you have the media bracelet, it's time to make friends with an official. The rest of the process involved in getting a competitor's bracelet is down to your own ingenuity, but it can be done.

CONTEST RULES

In both QS and CT surfing, priority reigns. It's the only time it does. Priority is basically a system where surfers in man-on-man heats take it in turns to catch waves, and don't have to fight for them. At the start of the heat, once the first wave has been ridden, the other surfer gets automatic priority.

Coloured discs at the event site indicate priority. Just look at the discs, displayed on poles so that the surfers in the water can clearly see what's happening, and make apparently knowledgeable comments about priority such as: 'Paddle away, Red. Don't let him sit on you with priority' or 'There are two waves coming through, Red. Watch him carefully on the first one because he's going to try and snooker you on both.' People in the immediate vicinity will look at you with newfound respect.

JUDGES

A panel of five judges assesses the waves the surfers ride in their heats on a scale of one to ten. It is obviously not that necessary to be a competent surfer in order to judge surfing.

Judging criteria includes the following:

- Commitment and degree of difficulty
- Innovative and progressive manoeuvres
- Combination of major manoeuvres
- Variety of manoeuvres
- Speed, power and flow.

Bluffers are unlikely to be familiar with any of these criteria, but no matter. If the subject comes up, simply show your mastery of the judging process by pointing out that surfers need to choose their waves carefully, because it's not about quantity – but quality.

It is obviously not that necessary to be a competent surfer in order to judge surfing.

It is also important to note that many judges – who make decisions that can and do affect surfers' careers, lives, relationships and attitudes to alcohol and sleeping tablets – do not even surf themselves, or only very rarely.

The head judge
The head judge presides over the panel and has the power to override any decisions it has made. The head judge also gets paid more for his work and usually gets better food and board as well. With the head judge having the final decision on everything, some people think that the rest of the panel is superfluous (except, of course, the judges themselves). When a head judge overrides a decision, the other judges sometimes argue their point. Although they have zero chance of winning such an argument, it does help them to justify their jobs to themselves.

WORLD CHAMPIONS
For the first decade of this millennium, three surfers with 16 titles between them dominated the male tour: Kelly Slater from Cocoa Beach in Florida with 11; Mick Fanning from Australia with two; and Andy Irons from Kauai in Hawaii with three. Before these title-holders, there were a multitude of world champions going back all the way to 1976, but few surfers can count that far. Since then the men's tour has seen the inexorable rise of the Hawaiian surfer John John Florence (*see* page 112) and the women's tour has been effectively the personal playground of Australian surfers since 1998 with Layne Beachley winning six consecutive titles between 1998 and 2003 and again in 2006. Her fellow Aussie Stephanie Gilmore also won six between 2007 and 2014, and the dominant female surfer of the current era is Tyler Wright. She is also Australian.

Slater, the man with the most titles, is also an actor (allegedly) and had a part in *Baywatch*. He played a professional surfer called Jimmy Slade and while his acting didn't win him too many glowing critical reviews (with more than one surf magazine commenting that to call it wooden would be an insult to trees), he did end up dating Pamela Anderson.

Andy Irons, or AI as he was affectionately known, died from an alleged drug overdose in 2010 aged 32. You need to know this. You also need to know that the world champion in 2012 was Joel 'Parko' Parkinson, an Australian contemporary (and childhood friend) of Mick Fanning, whose first victory at the ripe old age of 31 pleased a lot of people – especially those over 30.

AMATEUR SURFING

You might decide to rein in your bluffing, and say modestly that, although you 'could have made it on The Grind', you decided to adhere to the purer Corinthian spirit as an amateur. Many surf schools the world over have surfing leagues, and there are also clubs and amateur associations where one can surf against fellow members and possibly have a beer and a chat afterwards – a bit like club rugby but without the homo-erotic wrestling and drinking competitions.

If a surfer is coming up through the amateur ranks and realises that he or she has a shot at being a successful pro surfer then it is usually a quick and easy decision to turn pro. There is a lot of money to be made from pro surfing, and the sooner you make the move the sooner you can get your hands on a share of the loot. You will say that you had such an opportunity, but declined it on the grounds that you surf for the love it – not for the cold, hard cash.

PROFESSIONAL HANGERS-ON

Caddies

A number of pro surfers use caddies when the waves get big. A caddy sits in the channel with a spare board in case the surfer breaks his board while competing. If a surfer breaks his board, the caddy has to paddle to the spot where the surfer is swimming around. This is usually right where the biggest waves are breaking. The caddy then has to give the surfer the new board, and swim in.

Caddies are not allowed to have caddies themselves, despite their fairly constant requests for them. Caddies are usually either a surfer's very good friend, or reasonably unintelligent friend. They are all good swimmers.

Commentators

When a pro event rolls into town, there is always going to be a large percentage of spectators who don't understand that much about professional surfing. In order to educate them and keep them on the beach, the event sponsors generally employ a couple of commentators to keep everyone informed as to what is going on in the waves, as well as to inform the (often innumerate) contestants themselves of:

1. their actual scores, and

2. what scores they need in order to beat their opponents.

Commentators are well known for saying, at the start of pretty much every single wave ridden in a contest, 'Red (replace with whatever colour vest is being worn) up and riding' or 'Red on a fine-looking wave'. For some reason they don't seem to get tired of these phrases. Not unnaturally, everyone else does.

Commentators are usually ex-professional surfers and ex-world champions who have realised at the last minute that there is no life after pro surfing or being a world champ other than joining the media swamp as a commentator or analyst. Commentating may be considered a fairly lowly occupation within the surf industry, but ex-pros are ideally qualified to commentate. When doing so, they're almost certainly thinking, 'If only I had invested some of my prize money in property instead of spending it on parties, liquor and good-looking women/men,' while saying, 'And Red is up and riding, ladies and gentlemen. That's Red on a fine-looking wave.'

When the waves are really poor, it is up to the commentators to inject some life into a contest with anecdotes and facts about the surfers taking part. When the waves are really good no one cares what is being said, so the commentators usually talk louder and louder, or, to be heard above the roar of the waves, shout into their mics until someone complains. Then they sulk, clam up, and no one knows who is in the next heat.

Surf photographers

Though they are, in general, honest people trying to do an honest day's work, many people look at surf photographers a little suspiciously. In this male-dominated, outwardly heterosexual surfing world, the goal of the photographer is to take photos of mostly male surfers in various tropical and exotic locales, in numerous forms of undress from their low-slung, brightly coloured board shorts to their snug, revealing rubber second skins, and have them snapped up by surf magazines. The uber-masculine surf magazine industry can't get enough of such shots to reproduce in glossy format for other (mostly male) readers to buy. These photos, while being traded as high-action sports images, are really pretty calendar boy semi-nudes. OK, let's not go there…

Surf journalists

The lowliest of the lot, surf journalists are little more than the bottom-feeders of the surf industry. This is because they usually have no formal education behind them, let alone any sort of journalism degree or diploma, and make their money by writing about the mess-ups of professional surfers on or off the tour.

To make their stories more exciting and saleable, journalists often make up content as they go along, gleefully revealing the 'secrets' of pro surfers like their possible drug problems, their infidelities or their alcohol dependency. They are loathed by all surfers. However, if the surfers don't treat them with utmost respect, the journalists may (and most probably will) write even more unpleasant things about them. Many a surf hack has been castigated for writing damaging pro-surfer exposés but they are generally too thick-skinned to worry about the effects on their own reputations.

Surf journalists can be found hanging out at the VIP section of a surf contest area, scoring the free food and propping themselves up at the bar all day under the guise of 'research'. They eventually find themselves horribly exposed when they attempt to infiltrate the world of real journalism and are shown up as not knowing the difference between a preposition and a participle, and are then forced back to familiar lowbrow subject matter – surf journalism. Nonetheless, because of their skills at fabricating and embellishing, they can find themselves offered well-remunerated positions as 'director of communications' inside large surf companies' marketing departments. Sometimes they even get jobs writing *Bluffer's Guides*.

SPONSORS

You need to know how sponsorship works so you can offer advice to young, impressionable surfers (especially those of the opposite sex) and pick up any freebies on offer. There are two types of sponsors:

1. The event sponsor

The CT only has a handful of named sponsors paying for all their events – usually one of the very big international surf clothing companies. This is good news for the bluffer because, should you manage to get a media bracelet (on your way to a competitor's bracelet entailing a hedonistic overdose of a never-experienced-before level), there will also be a clothing pack from the relevant sponsor.

2. The personal sponsors

Most professionals have at least surfboard and clothing sponsors, with additional brands depending on the surfer, his or her build, looks and attitude. Naturally, you must claim that at your 'peak' you were deluged with offers from all of them.

If your audience shows sufficient interest, it might be necessary to pretend to know how to acquire sponsors. This is all you need to know:

1. Identify a company with which to start a mutually beneficial relationship. It benefits from having you represent it, and you benefit from taking its money.

2. Set up a meeting.

Prepare some clearly defined goals in your head, as well as a good CV consisting of past results and all relevant media coverage. Of course, you will have neither. But only you know that.

ETIQUETTE AND TRADITION

ETIQUETTE

There are many things that are said and many things that should remain unsaid in the water, especially if you are a visitor to a surf spot that has a strong local surfing community.

The question, 'Are you going for a surf?', for example, isn't going to win you many friends if someone is halfway through wriggling into his or her gear. You're most likely to get a sneering, 'No, I'm off to milk a cow in a rubber wetsuit' type of answer. Similarly, if someone is walking down to the water's edge with their surfboard and you ask the same question, don't be surprised if you get something like: 'No, I'm taking my board for a walk.' Either way, you're going to sound like an idiot, which is not the vibe you want. Rather, observe for a while and look for the right people to talk to. Questions like 'How are the waves?' or 'Did you get a few?' work fine and are innocuous enough, and don't really leave you open to searching scrutiny.

But when it comes to the etiquette of catching waves, you need to know that there is an intricate ranking system at play in the water and should familiarise yourself with the rules to avoid confrontation. Bluffers abhor confrontation.

The two basic rules of surfing etiquette are:

1. Surfers take it in turns for waves.

2. The person closest to the breaking part of the wave has right of way.

On the face of it, this is a simple enough system, but it is actually very complicated because human nature dictates that people do not like to wait in turn, especially if they feel any sense of entitlement, which many local surfers do. To speed things up, these surfers jump the queue and push close to the breaking part of the wave. This gives them, in their eyes, full rights to the next wave.

It's a hard system to get the hang of and a selfish surfer can cause the whole thing to break down. If there is a really greedy and aggressive person in the water it is pointless to argue, and better to paddle in and wait for a quieter time. Even if you fancy your chances in a polite exchange of views, this type of person has an IQ smaller than a goldfish and would interpret your attempt to point out his unreasonableness as a lack of 'respect'. His preferred response would be to insert his board into your mouth – sideways.

Never borrow someone's towel.
A beach towel is sacred.

If you have taken to the waves in order to enhance your bluffing credentials, here are some tips to earn the respect of other surfers in the water:

- If you have had a few waves, and someone else isn't catching many, give a wave away. Set someone up for a ride. Be generous, and don't make a big issue about it. Surfers are on the whole not generous, and this will make a big impression.

- Similarly, if there are surfers in the water who are less fit or competent than you, give them a few waves as well. This usually applies to older surfers and to female surfers of all ages. Help them along. Share the love. Who knows, that old guy floundering in the water might just catch the wave of his life and be that brewery-owning billionaire with a good-looking daughter who believes in imaginative sex on first dates.

- Don't shout when surfing. Some people shout at other surfers whom they either like or dislike, shout at themselves when they miss a wave, shout at their surfboards when they deem that their equipment has let them down, and just generally shout at nature, seagulls and other stuff. No one likes a shouter. Surfing is being at one with nature; it is riding on God's soul. The only sound should be that of breaking surf. On the other hand, no one likes a hippy either.

- Never borrow someone's towel to change or to dry off. A beach towel is sacred.

SURFING TRADITIONS

INITIATION RITES

There are some great traditions in surfing. One of them is about keeping the kids in line.

Youngsters who are taking up the sport are called 'grommets' (as opposed to kids who start bodyboarding and are immediately dubbed 'speed bumps'), and they have to go through certain rites of passage.

Carrying across a crowded room a beer bottle covered in Deep Heat while firmly wedged in a very private orifice is one particularly uncomfortable initiation rite, as is the somewhat bizarre blindfolding of said youngster and making him or her stick a finger in a pre-prepared orange filled with shoe polish. The history behind this one has been long forgotten, although the look on the victim's face when the orange is hidden from view and the blindfold removed always gets a good laugh, no matter how many times you've seen it.

In the old days, young surfers used to go through such traumas on a daily basis. Today's traditions of grommethood are rather more mundane.

REMEMBRANCE PADDLE OUT

A fairly serious tradition for the 'send-off' of a dead surfer, it involves family and friends paddling out to the departed surfer's favourite wave, forming a circle in the water on their boards, and then spreading the ashes and saying a few words plus a quick prayer to bid bon voyage.

It is always emotional, and hardcore, image-conscious surfers frequently weep unashamedly. Finally, all the surfers splash the water before breaking up the circle and heading for the waves. Then, if the waves are good, they carry on as usual with snaking, dropping in on each other, stealing each other's waves, threatening each other and generally paying their respects in the way the departed would have wanted. It's a great tradition.

FIRST TIMES

There are a number of 'first times' that surfers have to go through in their quest to become competent. These have become traditions that are often brought up as topics of conversation when the waves are flat or when the beer is flowing, so it's a good idea for the bluffer to rehearse a few foolproof 'first-time' stories for instant credibility.

The first time you bought a real surfboard is a great tale. 'It was in terrible condition with a single broken fin and held together by duct tape. But it was mine, it was my first, I loved it, and it became an extension of me, etc.' (Don't go on too much; even the most forgiving audience has its limits.)

The first time you got inside the spinning vortex of a wave and got 'tubed' is also a significant step towards becoming a true surfer. Every surfer can remember his or her first tube (*see* Glossary).

The first time you had a really bad wipeout and 'nearly drowned' is also a typically uplifting story and is fertile territory for plenty of embellishment and exaggeration, as long as it stays within the realms of possibility; no one is going to believe that you paddled out alone in 20-foot waves for your first surf. A bluffer needs to build reality into such a story, using believable elements like eight-foot surf, a big set, a nasty wipeout, rocks and seeing stars – all equally plausible.

Shark stories are also acceptable currency (but can become self-fulfilling prophecies, so be careful), as are getting caught in currents and heading out into the shipping lanes. At sunset. You might find that if your audience has had a few beers and is not concentrating that hard anymore, you can get away with using terms like 'bone-dry reef', 'such an irresistible wave that my instinct took over and I paddled for it anyway', or 'I was held under for so long that the water was black. I didn't know which way was up, my life flashed before me, and

I saw a bright light under the water that seemed to be beckoning me.'

(Note: The 'bright light' story should only be used at the end of a drinking session when no one is going to remember a word that was said. Make sure that no one is recording with a mobile phone or similar, because no surfer would be caught dead talking about being nearly dead. It's bad karma.)

Honesty can enhance a bluffer's credibility immeasurably. Simply say something like: 'I got really chewed up by that one. I don't fancy going through it again.' Then, chewing your lip thoughtfully, look nobly into the far distance and refuse to elaborate.

There comes a time for every surfer when he or she is faced with big waves. Your first time paddling out in surf that is bigger than you're accustomed to defines your attitude to big waves from that day forth. Giant swells incite a fight-or-flight syndrome; you will either puff up with adrenaline and attack the waves with gusto or will deflate in fear, looking for a smaller wave to come in as soon as possible, and do the walk of shame up the beach in front of everyone who might be tempted to level accusations of chickening out (with appropriate clucking noises). Your best approach is to explain sorrowfully but stoically that you were a fearless big-wave surfer in your youth until 'that giant north swell of '98, the biggest surf ever seen in that part of the world'. There is no harm in admitting that you haven't been quite the same since. Honesty can enhance a bluffer's credibility immeasurably. Simply say something like: 'I got really chewed up by that one. I don't fancy going through it again.' Then, chewing your lip thoughtfully, look nobly into the far distance and refuse to elaborate.

SHARKS

Shark tales are a very important part of the surfing tradition, and it is important that you should know something about them. All experienced surfers profess to respect the mighty predators – and you should be no exception.

The best shark tale of recent years concerns a guy named Doug Niblack who was surfing 50 yards off the Oregon coast in the USA. He felt his longboard hit something in the water and suddenly found himself riding on the back of a great white, with a dorsal fin directly in front of his feet. He estimated that the ride lasted no more than four seconds before the shark went out from under him, dragging him for a short distance by his ankle tether. The incident might have been dismissed as a completely unbelievable bluff had it not been witnessed by an off-duty US Coast Guard officer surfing nearby.

This is undoubtedly a good story, but beware of repeating it with you playing the leading role. All surfers love a good shark story, and they're likely to have heard this one.

Nevertheless, it is traditional to discuss sharks, so you must arm yourself with the following facts:

1. Sharks are misunderstood. Human beings are not their preferred food source. They prefer sea lions and seals (much more blubbery and nourishing) and most shark attacks are the result of mistaken identity. So if you happen to resemble a sea lion or a seal, don't go surfing. Take up another sport.

2. Sharks have made the sea their home for more than 400 million years. It stopped being our home at roughly the same time that the first vertebrates crawled up the beaches and decided that a shark-free environment was preferable.

If a shark were to kill you, it's really nothing personal.

---

3. Out of 360 species of sharks, only four of them are likely to be responsible for unprovoked attacks on humans: the great white, the bull, the tiger and the oceanic whitetip. There is no truth in the frequently repeated assumption that the bigger the shark, the more dangerous it is. The biggest sharks are a danger only to plankton. So if you resemble plankton, again, don't go surfing.

4. The chances of being attacked by a shark are very low. Only a small percentage of shark species are

known to frequent waters within paddling distance of a coast. Very few of these are likely to attack surfers. In fact, the chances of being attacked by a shark were estimated recently at one in more than 11 million (admittedly higher if you're a surfer). The chances of actually dying from a shark attack are one in more than 260 million.

5. Look at it from the shark's point of view. They're inquisitive creatures. If they spot something they don't recognise, they sometimes 'test bite' it. If they had fingers, they'd probably squeeze it, but they haven't so they can't. And so people might get bitten from time to time. But you should always emphasise in any shark discussion that the sea is their home, and if you should suffer the ultimate price for entering it uninvited, then you wouldn't want your host to be hunted down and turned into soup or a necklace. Despite the best efforts of films like *Jaws* to tell you otherwise, if a shark were to kill you, it's really nothing personal.

SURF ON CELLULOID

Whenever and wherever surfers congregate to swap stories about their professed knowledge of the sport and its culture, the conversation will inevitably turn to a long cinematic tradition which has provided the world of the moving image with hundreds of surfing movies. Most of them are instantly forgettable, but a precious few earn a place alongside the best of other sporting documentaries and film dramas.

This is prime bluffing territory, because very few surfers will have seen all of the best known examples of the genre. Neither, of course, will you – but you will nonetheless have the priceless advantage of having just enough knowledge of each to convince your keenly receptive listeners that you are a genuine surf movie aficionado with a depth of insight that demands instant respect and admiration.

Any dialogue on the subject should start with the compelling observation that the very first surfing film was the work of the prolific American inventor Thomas Edison in 1906 at Waikiki Beach in Honolulu, Hawaii.

More than a dozen native surfers can clearly be seen riding gentle offshore rollers in fetching early 20th-century one-piece tanksuits. In fact it is unlikely that Edison himself was behind this particular motion picture camera (which naturally he had invented). At the time, you might casually mention, he was working extensively with the noted Victorian cinematographer Robert K Bonine, who he had commissioned to shoot an 'actuality' film (documentary) about life in the Polynesian islands. Don't make the mistake of committing yourself to who was holding the camera, but simply make the point that the film is more important than such trifles as who was actually cranking the handle.

This unique glimpse of a new sport in the nascent stages of its development (now freely available on the internet) led to a proliferation of surf movies, albeit not for another half a century. At the beginning they were mainly documentaries featuring healthy, athletic, sun-bronzed, scantily clad young people having a lovely time splashing about in the surf, but then increasingly filmmakers began to see the dramatic potential of a lifestyle which celebrated a sense of freedom, adventure, and living the dream.

The following surf movies are in order of date of release:

GIDGET (1959)

A wholesome teenage girl discovers beach life, and proves to be a natural surfer after initially being scorned by her male contemporaries who treat her with knee-jerk scepticism (for which read 'sexism') and nickname her 'Gidget' (a contraction of 'Girl' and 'Midget', for which read sexism and heightism). Along the way she gets a sun tan, an education, and falls in love, proving that women, unlike men, are more than capable of multi-tasking. All-American Sandra Dee plays the lead role opposite James Darren ('Moondoggie') and Cliff Robertson ('The Big Kahuna'), both of whom look like they've been dipped in a barrel of Cuprinol. The film was the first of a series following Gidget's further adventures, and became a box office hit.

WHAT TO SAY: 'Easy to sneer at, but in fact a significant moment in the birth of the surf-movie genre. One unexpected consequence was the creation in 1962 of *Surfer* magazine, whose publisher John Severson was motivated by a desire to counter what he saw as the negative effects of the popularisation of surfing by the *Gidget* film series.'

THE ENDLESS SUMMER (1966)

This is the one that every surfing bluffer really needs to know about, and which is still unrivalled as the most iconic surfing documentary of all time. Two young Californian surfers follow an endless summer around the world in an epic journey to find the holy grail of waves. They eventually find it off Cape St Francis in South Africa, a classic barrelling right-hander in perfect conditions and – crucially – with the right director, Bruce

Brown, behind the camera. Brown, who did much of the filming from his own board, is the first name to drop in any discussion about surf films, and the only word to drop is 'transformative'. The film was actually finished in 1964, but Brown couldn't find a distributor. It took two years more to attract critical attention when Brown borrowed everything he could to hire a movie theatre in Manhattan. The film subsequently grossed $30million worldwide.

WHAT TO SAY: 'What Bruce Brown did, and what nobody has done since, was to square the circle. He was able to present surfing as it really is, to non-surfers.' (*The Encyclopedia of Surfing*).

FIVE SUMMER STORIES (1972)

It would be odd to compile a list of some of the most memorable surf movies of all time without a soundtrack featuring a track by the Beach Boys. Fortunately this cult classic has one, if only one, with the song 'Pipeline' accompanying a surfer's elegant slo-mo glide down the full length of a barrel in glorious Technicolor. It's a perfect partnership, and begs the question why more surf movies haven't taken full advantage of a particularly individual sound which could have been tailor-made for the sport. Meanwhile, the film has no narrative and no plot. Yet it still manages to pull in reviews along the lines of 'the finest surf movie ever made...a cultural icon, a time capsule from a watershed era when the world was at a critical crossroads.'

WHAT TO SAY: 'Spellbinding. But it would have been even better with the Beach Boys providing the full soundtrack.'

CRYSTAL VOYAGER (1973)

The main thing you'll need to know about this Australian surfing documentary was that it was the first to take its audience actually inside the tube (the inside of a breaking wave, *see* Glossary). This was made possible by advanced photographic technology, otherwise known as a camera sealed within a rudimentary waterproof housing worn by US surfer-filmmaker George Greenough on his back. Bluffers should also know that much of the soundtrack was provided courtesy of Pink Floyd.

WHAT TO SAY: 'Of course, one of the most interesting and somewhat unintended consequences of the film was to make the "kneeboard" almost acceptable to purists, especially if it happened to be of the "spoon" variety favoured by Greenough.' (*See* Glossary)

BIG WEDNESDAY (1978)

Mix surfing and Vietnam and, no, you don't automatically get the infamous surfing under mortar fire scene in *Apocalypse Now*. You also get this coming of age movie recounting the efforts of three friends to avoid growing up by trying to ensure that their passion for surfing (and sex) is uninterrupted and kept firmly at the forefront of their lives. Unfortunately the Vietnam War gets in the way and, if not actually depicted in its usual visceral brutality, it hovers in the wings like a spectre at the feast. Towards the end of the movie the trio of friends is reunited in plenty of time to enjoy a good surfing session, and to reflect on the loss of innocence.

WHAT TO SAY: 'The "Big Wednesday", which has nothing to do with the day of the week, is a metaphor for life – the time when the biggest, bluest, most powerful wave of a lifetime rolls in and demands that a surfer prove that he or she has what it takes to surmount it.'

POINT BREAK (1991)

A film involving an FBI agent on the trail of a bank robbing surfer gang with a penchant for wearing face masks depicting former US presidents sounds like a less than promising plot line. But *Point Break* nonetheless became a cult classic. Bluffers need to know that director Kathryn Bigelow went on to direct Oscar-winning *The Hurt Locker*, so she knows a thing or two about spinning a yarn. Starring Keanu Reeves and Patrick Swayze who both took surfing lessons before filming began, most of the more technically demanding scenes were filmed using stunt double pro-surfers. The best known of these was Darrick Doerner, a legendary big wave specialist who fills in for Swayze in the final scene as (spoiler alert!) he chooses to take the ultimate ride into a watery death rather than spend the rest of his life behind bars.

WHAT TO SAY: 'More than 25 years after it was filmed, no other film has come close to setting a crime thriller successfully in the world of surfing (although the 2015 sequel, also called *Point Break*, was arguably a crime in itself).'

BLUE CRUSH (2002)

The striking promo poster for the film features an attractively toned and tanned young woman (Kate Bosworth) in a bikini looking every inch beach-board-body-ready. This isn't the best scripted or best acted movie in cinema history, but neither is it the worst. The real winners are the cameras and the people behind them. Some of the sumptuous visuals take the breath away, and that's just the surf and scenery. The plot is simple enough: girl is a great surfer, girl wipes out and nearly drowns, girl falls in love with prime piece of footballing beefcake, girl has to get her confidence back to enter a surf competition at Pipeline, on Hawaii's North Shore (*see* page 40), girl wipes out in first heat, girl catches the best wave of the day in the second. Guess what happens?

WHAT TO SAY: 'Don't be tempted to go overboard about all the surf-candy on display. There's some serious wave riding by expert women pros going on in the background.'

RIDING GIANTS (2004)

Another of the must-see documentaries, this is the definitive account of the origins and history of big wave surfing with a particular focus on the pioneers who helped to make it one of the great adrenaline sports. Bluffers will claim to have viewed it on numerous occasions to help iron out a few glitches in their technique, but the real lure is the spectacular action footage of riding enormous waves in such big wave meccas as Mavericks, Pipeline, Maui, and Teahuppo. There's also plenty of dramatic footage of wipeouts in massive walls of water, which you might modestly concede have occasionally featured in your own recent experience. Of course the truth is that a cinema screen is as close as you're likely to get to any wave bigger than a ripple.

WHAT TO SAY: 'There's no point in being there if you don't go for it. I've been blown out of enough kegs to know that there's only one way in, and one way out.'

SOUL SURFER (2011)

The uplifting true story of the remarkable Bethany Hamilton, a champion 13-year-old Hawaiian surfer with briny in her veins who loses her arm in an attack by a 14ft tiger shark and overcomes seemingly insuperable odds to continue to compete at the highest level. There are considerable hurdles along the way, but she refuses to give in and meets them head on with unwavering self-belief and good old Christian faith. The film could have been a ghastly Hollywood confection of mawkish sentimentality, but turns out to be an inspiring account about how no challenge is too big to be faced down. AnnaSophia Robb acquits herself in the main role with skill and credibility, with Hamilton filling in as her body double in some of the more technically demanding scenes.

WHAT TO SAY: (adopting suitably lofty tone): 'Young or old, we could all learn from Bethany's courage, strength, perseverance, dedication… (and as many other suitable superlatives that spring to mind).

CHASING MAVERICKS (2012)

Another true(ish) biopic about a teenage boy, Jay Moriarity, who lives within walking distance of one of the planet's most notorious waves and determines to ride it by enlisting the help of grizzled local surfer-philosopher, Frosty Hesson (played by Scottish actor Gerard Butler). He is put through a rigorous training regime, including an eye-popping attempt to hold his breath for four minutes, and finally takes on the brute known as Mavericks, remorselessly crashing onto the coast of California. In so doing, he makes the cover of *Surfer* magazine with a memorable wipeout which serves only to strengthen his resolve to ride the wave successfully. Of course, eventually he does. Sadly, however, he didn't live long enough to realise his undoubted potential as a pro surfer, and died aged 22 in a freediving accident in the Indian Ocean. The 'paddle out' (*see* page 85) in his memory was one of the biggest ever seen in the US and is recreated at the end of the film.

WHAT TO SAY: (quoting Frosty's opening lines): 'We all come from the sea, but we are not all of the sea. Those of us who are, we children of the tides, must return to it again and again...'

If you can remember this, it's bluffing gold.

HAVE BOARD, WILL TRAVEL

Surf travel is one of the greatest things in a surfer's life. But the rules are not weighted in the surfer's favour. In surf travel, you go halfway around the world, paying punishing excess baggage charges for your boards, while vast collections of other sporting paraphernalia travel for free.

BOARD PACKING

There are two clear schools of thought when it comes to packing boards for air travel:

1. Go to great lengths to cover your board in bubble wrap and expensive board covers made of Kevlar.

2. Pack your board more lightly, adding 'CAUTION: FRAGILE' stickers to try to persuade baggage handlers not to chuck them out of the hold.

Either way, your boards will be chucked out of the hold. If they don't get damaged on the plane, they will certainly get damaged once the handlers see them; it's a personal challenge to their absolute right to destroy any passenger's baggage which looks as if it might be worth something. Even if they remain intact during the flight or at the airport, they'll probably get destroyed when they fly off the hire car that doesn't have the roof rack you pre-booked. It's a hopeless situation. There is no simple solution, except to carry them by hand.

Pile three or more friends, some money, some booze, camping equipment and surfboards into a knackered old truck or station wagon and point it at the coast. Waves are a nice bonus, but not a prerequisite.

THE ROAD TRIP

It is absolutely imperative that bluffers are familiar with the lazy, hazy folklore of the road trip. It is a right of passage for surfers, an essential part of the sport's culture. Pile three or more friends, some money, some booze, camping equipment and surfboards into a knackered old truck or station wagon and point it at the coast. Waves are a nice bonus, but not a prerequisite.

It is essential that the trip has some form of illegal, immoral or improper component in its make-up – like an unroadworthy car, a driver without a licence, a member of the crew who is MIA (missing in action – i.e., from work), or someone who has a 'special friend' down the coast that his wife or girlfriend doesn't know about.

There is always plenty of bad behaviour associated with a road trip. The crew of a 'surf chariot' must always be of the same gender, i.e., all girls or all boys. Mixed groups, families and engaged or married couples don't go on road trips; it's just not done. The close human proximity involved is too grim for most opposite-sex parties to handle. So you should take careful note of the vital role of the road trip and equip yourself with a suitable story, such as the armed Mozambique police officer whom you plied with marijuana cookies, the Mexican border guards you bribed with pornographic magazines, the time you conned your way into a restricted West African diamond mining zone to ride a perfect wave…just let your imagination fly like a board on a breaking 25-foot wave.

LOCALISM

You need to be aware of this term for describing hostile behaviour to out-of-towners at certain surf spots around the world. Some, like one of the Barras in Mexico or Third Dip in Hawaii, are practically no-go areas in this respect. Often rearing its ugly head when the surf gets crowded, localism is a really unwelcome feature of the sport, much like genital wetsuit rash.

In its most ignorant manifestation, localism means that local residents feel that they have more rights to the waves than non-locals. In its most deeply unattractive form, it means banning from the surf anyone who isn't local by means of punching them on the nose, letting down tyres, breaking fins and, in rare cases, defecating on car windscreens and bonnets – a real bummer when it gets baked on by a boiling sun.

Localism should be roundly condemned by bluffers at every opportunity. Except to those who practise it, especially if there are more of them than you.

WAVES OF HILARITY

Yes, surfers do indeed see the funny side to life. In fact, a large part of a surfer's life is spent laughing his or her head off, usually at the misfortune of others. You could call it 'surfing *Schadenfreude*', which you might remember to mention to a knuckle-dragging, no-necked, shallow-browed localist just to watch their bovine features contort with incomprehension. Surfers like to laugh a lot. So you need to know where and when to join in, and what is acceptable to laugh about.

A fellow surfer going 'over the falls' is probably the funniest thing a surfer can witness. A big wave comes in and your fellow surfer is in a good position to paddle for and catch it. It quickly becomes obvious that it is a serious wave, though, bigger than expected, and the surfer paddling for it has a good chance of coming unstuck. Still, you cheer him or her on with full-throated encouragement, whooping and screaming things like, 'Go for it!' and 'Wave of the day!', in the certain knowledge that the wave will break quicker than expected, leaving the surfer stuck within the falling lip and going over with the lip as it breaks. (It's funny just thinking about it.)

Consumed with anxiety about the dangers of what could be lying beneath (a fellow surfer, a shallow reef, a shark…), and sheer helplessness, the surfer is at the mercy of Huey (*see* Glossary). This form of wipeout is the funniest thing for a surfer to watch from the safety of the channel or the beach. Nothing gets a group of surfers cackling with laughter like watching a surfer going over the falls on a seriously big wave. What makes it even more hilarious is the expression of absolute terror on the face of the doomed surfer while going over. Bluffers should try to maintain an air of gravitas in these circumstances, but laughter is a very contagious force.

The over-the-falls spectacle is made better by the style and method of the wipeout. For instance, once it has been ascertained that there is a disaster looming, the hapless surfer sometimes turns around to pull out of the wave. This often results in the surfer going over the falls backwards. (That's even funnier.)

Sometimes the surfer is seen scrambling to his feet, but then gets knocked down by the wave and goes flying over the falls on his knees. (Funnier still.)

But the high point of the humour has to be when the surfer eventually rises to the surface with pieces of broken board floating about, completely dazed for a moment, and has enough time to look relieved before a second wave pounds down with the force of a sledgehammer and sends him for one more turn around the saltwater spin cycle. (Absolutely hilarious.)

The other most comical scene in the water is the 'caught-inside' situation. This is when a surfer in dramatically big surf decides to sit closer to the breaking wave than other surfers in an act of bravery or folly. Sitting closer can either result in the surfer catching an absolute pearler of a wave in front of the other surfers (not so funny – in fact, deeply irritating), or in a massive wave breaking on the head of the surfer before he can react. (This is hugely satisfying.)

The scream of a trapped surfer in these circumstances will evoke peals of laughter from those in the safety of the peanut gallery.

Sometimes, a surfer who is caught inside will scream in fear as he suddenly sees the massive mountain of moving water and knows he has no chance to avoid it. The scream of a trapped surfer in these circumstances will evoke peals of laughter from those in the safety of the peanut gallery.

And then, on occasion, a surfer will panic when faced with a caught-inside situation and will do something ill-advised like trying to catch the white water by lying down on the board. This is impossible to do because the wave will be travelling at such speed that it will just swallow anything in its path. When a surfer tries this stunt, there will be more roars of laughter. Bluffers are unlikely ever to find themselves 'caught inside', but should nevertheless know one of the safest methods of dealing with such a situation: stand on your board while facing the wave and use it as a platform to dive and gain some depth to escape the foaming turbulence above.

The surfing tribe the world over has a simple golden rule: always surf with a friend so you have someone to laugh at.

Should a surfer slip while attempting this manoeuvre, the last thing he will hear before a giant wave knocks him over like a rag doll and thrashes him to within an inch of his life will be his friends, his lifelong buddies, screaming with pent-up laughter at his impending doom. The surfing tribe the world over has a simple golden rule: always surf with a friend so you have someone to laugh at.

NAME-DROPPING

Some major names in surfing are bound to come up on a fairly regular basis, and if you're to hold your own in any conversation about the sport, you're really going to have to know some (and preferably all) of the following…

KELLY SLATER

Florida-born Kelly Slater is the most successful male surfer of all time, winning 11 world titles between 1992 and 2011. At the age of 20 he became the youngest world champion in history, and at 39, the oldest. Apart from his role as Jimmy Slade in 27 episodes of *Baywatch* in the early 1990s, and notable appearances in many surfing documentaries, all that is really necessary to know is that in 2010 the US House of Representatives honoured him for his 'outstanding and unprecedented achievements in the world of surfing and for being an ambassador of the sport and excellent role model'. Nothing further to add, except that his remarkable record is never likely to be beaten. You can claim to have surfed with him – everybody else does.

WAYNE 'RABBIT' BARTHOLOMEW

Former world champion in 1978, devotee of carrots (hence the sobriquet) and former president of the Association of Surfing Professionals, Rabbit successfully steered the professional side of the sport in the right direction. In his youth, he used to win eating contests; since then he has survived both cancer and having his teeth punched out because he had too much to say about Australians being better surfers than Hawaiians. Not a good idea when you're an Australian addressing a group of Hawaiian surfers in Hawaii.

GREG NOLL

In 1969 Greg went out and surfed at Makaha in Hawaii during what has become known as 'the greatest swell of the twentieth century'. He caught what was then probably the biggest wave ever surfed (so described by those who saw it from a very safe distance). This was soon followed by the biggest ever wipeout. Noll never surfed again, and it took him a few years to speak about his experience. When he did, he wrote a book about it called *Da Bull: Life Over The Edge*. Later he became a prominent longboard shaper.

KEN BRADSHAW

This surfer from Texas also rewrote the record books when he was towed into the next biggest wave ever surfed at Outside Log Cabins in Hawaii in 1998. The wave was said to be 80 feet. Bradshaw went into a deep depression afterwards, claiming that his ultimate goal in life had been fulfilled and there was nothing else left. Then he fell in love with women's world champ Layne Beachley and felt better. Then she left him and he got depressed again.

GARRETT McNAMARA

Now in his 50s, McNamara is a big-wave veteran. The fearless American found arguably the biggest of his life in early 2013 in Nazaré, Portugal, when he got towed into a monstrous record-breaking near 100-footer which featured in photographs on the front pages of many newspapers around the world. His wife Nicole, with whom he had exchanged vows only months previously at the foot of the Nazaré lighthouse (dwarfed by the onrushing wave in the pictures), was quoted as saying: 'He is definitely not allowed to surf that spot again.' Garrett replied unconvincingly: 'I didn't realise where I was and I promised my wife I wouldn't surf there.' Viewers of his feat on YouTube will see just how close he came to disaster as the wave broke over him perilously close to the rocks.[1]

1. As this edition went to print, British big wave surfer Tom Butler, 29, had just successfully ridden what photographers and onlookers confirmed to be a record breaking wave of over 100 feet at Nazaré. The WSL is currently adjudicating his claim.

MARK RICHARDS

Australian legend Richards won four world surfing titles between 1979 and 1982, despite having one of the most curious, some say ugly, styles of surfing ever seen. It was once compared to a 'wounded seagull'.

BETHANY HAMILTON

This petite young blonde was attacked by a 14ft tiger shark while she was surfing in Hawaii in 2003, aged 13. It ripped her arm off just below the shoulder. Bethany survived, recovered, and went surfing again with one arm. It took her a little while to get her confidence back but she started competing again, and won a national title against two-armed opponents just two years after the injury. She went on to become a champion surfer and her story was the subject of a major Hollywood movie in 2011 called *Soul Surfer* (*see* page 98).

JOHN JOHN FLORENCE

The 26-year-old Hawaiian surfer was tipped as a world title contender while still in his teens, and fulfilled most expectations soon afterwards. He grew up in a house overlooking Banzai Pipeline and is recognised as one of the most dominant Pipeline surfers of his era, despite having broken his back on the wave in 2011. Undeterred, he won back to back world titles in 2016 and 2017. Don't be tempted to claim that you taught him everything he knows. He was first on a surfboard at six months and has been a sponsored athlete since he was six years old.

WENDY BOTHA

A former world surfing champion, South African-born Wendy won three world titles in the 1980s, and then again in 1992, but she is arguably more famous for her delightful photo spread in Australian *Playboy* in 1989, the magazine's first sell-out edition ever. She moved to Australia shortly afterwards where she became an Australian citizen. The jury is still out about whether she did the women's pro surfing community a disservice, or gave it a much needed shot in the arm. What is certain is that male surfers weren't complaining.

LAYNE BEACHLEY

Winning seven world titles between 1998 and 2006 makes Layne the most successful female surfer of all time. From Manly in Sydney, Australia, she famously challenged the late male world champion Andy Irons to a surf-off, convincing the world media that she would beat him. Everyone came to watch, and he won, as was rather expected. It is quite possible that she was distracted by her split with big wave surfer Ken Bradshaw, or maybe Irons decided that there was no way he was going to lose to a girl. Whatever, she was undeniably exceptional.

ß

There's no point in pretending that you know everything about surfing – nobody does – but if you've got this far and have absorbed at least a modicum of the information and advice contained within these pages, then you will almost certainly know 99% more than the rest of the human race does about what surfing is, where to do it and what to say about it. What you now do with this information is up to you, but here's a suggestion: be confident about your newfound knowledge, see how far it takes you, but above all, have fun using it. After all, you are now a bona fide expert in the art of bluffing about one of the world's coolest, most aspirational sports. Just remember not to try to put too much of what you've learnt into practice.

GLOSSARY

Air Riding off the top of a wave, travelling through the air and reconnecting with the wave to carry on with the ride. Also what there's all too little of when held underwater after a wipeout.

Bail out Vacating your board when the going gets decidedly hairy – usually when paddling out and about to be pulverised by a breaking wave.

Barrel One of many names for surfing's holy grail. Also known as 'tube' or 'keg', it's the hollow part of the wave formed by the top travelling faster than the bottom. The idea is that the surfer gets into the barrel and travels down it from one end to the other. Great for action shots.

Carve Turning a board on a wave. The smoother, longer and more graceful the better.

Cooking Everything looking very good for surfing. Very good conditions.

Cranking Everything looking equally good.

Caught inside When the roll of a giant wave catches you out of position and breaks on top of you – one of the scariest moments in surfing. Shaken surfers can be seen sobbing and glumly cleaning the seats of their wetsuits or board shorts afterwards.

Channel Deep-water gulley next to a reef or a sandbank where you can sit and shout encouragement to friends as they try to surf waves that are way out of their league. Also a deep groove on the underside of a surfboard which makes water flow along it and, in the process, increases the speed of the board. Probably a good idea for bluffers to apply some filler to slow it down.

Drilling To be propelled off a board unintentionally and firmly 'drilled' into the seabed or reef, head first into the water. Not a pleasant experience.

Dropping in Not a visit to friends or neighbours but the forbidden action of catching the same wave as another surfer when that surfer has the inside track. Cause of most of the animosity in surfing.

Frontside air reverse Travelling down a wave at good speed before launching into the air, spinning around through 360° before landing and continuing along the wave. Usually only achievable by the young and supple, or on rare occasions by bluffers who have absolutely no idea what is happening.

Full-rail carving Using your weight and the rails of the surfboard to turn the board gracefully as well as powerfully – a concept that is entirely alien to bluffers.

Gnarly a) a wave that is nasty, scary to look at and difficult to catch; b) an adjective used to describe a really rough-looking member of the opposite sex in a nightclub.

Goofy foot A term for describing which foot goes in front on a surfboard. In this case, it'll be your right one. If you're not sure which is 'right' and which is 'left', you probably shouldn't be on a surfboard. If in doubt about which foot you favour, get someone to push you from behind and notice which foot automatically goes in front first. A goofy foot is also known as a 'screw foot'. Note that a surfer who stands heavily on the board with both feet occupying the same place is sometimes known as a 'club foot'. Charming.

Grom/grommet An adolescent surfer, or an older one who has just started surfing, who established surfers are allowed to abuse without any fear of reprisal.

Gun Surfboard used for surfing big waves. Also known as a 'rhino-chaser', or a 'stick'. When the waves get really big, a good phrase for bluffers to use is, 'It looks like death on a stick out there' or, 'I left my gun at home so I can't go surfing today, although I really, really want to.' The problem is that if someone says that they have a spare gun in the car, you're in deep trouble.

Huey Australian pagan god of surfing, adopted by surfers worldwide. Whenever there is a period of no waves, surfers gather and pray to Huey and sometimes burn an old surfboard as a sacrifice. At Newquay's Fistral Beach in Cornwall, surfboard burning has been known to be a twice-daily occurrence.

Hussled/hassled When someone catches a wave that clearly belongs to you. Can be compared to stealing someone's beer or partner (in that order).

Kitesurfing A hybrid of surfing and flying a kite. No waves are necessary. All you need is wind, a power kite, and a board.

Kneeboarding A much derided variation of surfing where the rider stays on their knees. Provides more stability so useful if you're holding a camera.

Kook A surfer of below-average skills. Someone who is really struggling to grasp the basic fundamentals. Used to describe many international rugby players (but never to their faces) who surf for fitness.

Leash (aka 'kook cord') The lead that attaches your board to your ankle. Sometimes serves as an emergency device to tow cars out of the sand, to tie boards to roof racks or for mild S&M high jinks. Originally known as a 'dog leash', a surf leash can also be used to walk your dog.

Lineup A queue of surfers waiting to catch a good wave. Normal queue etiquette prevails. In other words there will always be those who observe it and those who ignore it.

Natural foot Opposite of goofy foot: when you stand with your left foot forward like the great majority of surfers, including most of the champions. Also known as 'regular foot'.

Off the lip A highly skilled manoeuvre where the surfer goes to the top of the wave and pivots on the lip. The idea is to go up as vertically as possible and turn as quickly as possible. The bluffer will claim to have perfected it.

Over the falls Going over with the falling lip of a breaking wave. You'd stand a better chance going over Niagara in a barrel.

Ripper Someone who surfs well. In surfing circles, it also describes an episode of especially loud and forceful flatulence.

Secret spot Surf spot known by few. The location of a secret spot is not revealed to anyone, not even a spouse or loved one. Bluffers should claim to have one, thus explaining why they are rarely seen in the water.

Snake To paddle around behind a surfer who is already in position and then steal his or her wave. Can be compared to unashamed queue-jumping in an airport or at a ski lift. One of the worst crimes in surfing.

Sock Nylon cover used to protect surfboards from the harsh sun. Can also double as a tight sleeping bag, or bodybag (*see* 'Over the falls').

Surf rage Outbreak of temper known to happen in intensely overcrowded surfing situations. Much like road rage, surf rage is punishable by law, but is usually dealt with on the beach, mano-a-mano.

Tube The inside of a breaking wave. The highest scored move in pro surfing is the tube ride. Also known as a 'barrel' (*see* page 115), it is supposed to be one of the more addictive elements of the sport, just behind ice-cold after-surf beers.

Wax Substance placed on the deck of a board for traction. Also used for writing 'Go Home Kook' on the cars of people who catch too many waves.

Windsurfing Keeping your balance standing on a board with a sail. Propelled by wind power. Nothing like as cool as wave power.

A BIT MORE BLUFFING...

Available from all good bookshops

bluffers.com